MAKING ROOM
FOR LEADERSHIP
POWER, SPACE AND INFLUENCE

MaryKate Morse
Foreword by **Leonard Sweet**

IVP Books

An imprint of InterVarsity Press
Downers Grove, Illinois

InterVarsity Press
P.O. Box 1400, Downers Grove, IL 60515-1426
World Wide Web: wwwivpress.com
E-mail: email@ivpress.com

InterVarsity Press® is the book-publishing division of InterVarsity Christian Fellowship/USA®, a student
movement active on campus at hundreds of universities, colleges and schools of nursing in the United
States of America, and a member movement of the International Fellowship of Evangelical Students.
For information about local and regional activities, write Public Relations Dept., InterVarsity Christian
Fellowship/USA, 6400 Schroeder Rd., P.O. Box 7895, Madison, WI 53707-7895, or visit the IVCF website
at <www.intervarsity.org>.

Scripture quotations, unless otherwise noted, are from the New Revised Standard Version of the Bible,
copyright 1989 by the Division of Christian Education of the National Council of the Churches of Christ
in the USA. Used by permission. All rights reserved.

The song "Mister Cellophane" (from Chicago), words by FRED EBB, music by JOHN KANDER is
©1975 (Renewed) KANDER-EBB INC. and UNICHAPPELL MUSIC INC. All rights administered by
UNICHAPPELL MUSIC INC. All rights reserved. Used by permission of ALFRED PUBLISHING CO., INC.

Design: Cindy Kiple
Images: David Marchal/iStockphoto

ISBN 978-0-8308-3448-8

Printed in the United States of America ∞

Library of Congress Cataloging-in-Publication Data

Morse, MaryKate, 1948-
   Making room for leadership: power, space and influence / MaryKate
   Morse
      p. cm.
   Includes biliographical references.
   ISBN 978-0-8308-3448-8 (pbk.: alk. paper)
   1. Influence (Psychology)—Religious aspects—Christianity. 2.
Persuasian (Psychology) 3. Leadership—Religious
aspects—Christianity. 4. Body language. 5. Personal space. 6.
Interpersonal relations—Religious aspects—Christianity. I. Title.
BV4597.53.I52M67 2008
253—dc22

                                                                    2008031404

P   23 22 21 20 19 18 17 16 15 14 13 12 11 10 9 8 7 6 5 4 3 2 1

Y   27 26 25 24 23 22 21 20 19 18 17 16 15 14 13 12 11 10 09 08

CONTENTS

To Lorraine, my stepmom,
deeply loved and carried in my heart

FOREWORD

A Matriculation in Sign School
Unearthing the Patter and the Patternings

Stephen King is one of the bestselling authors of all time. He is known for his ability to tell stories (especially horror stories) in both print and film that pull you in until you almost can't get out. But Stephen King denies that he creates these stories. In fact, he contends that no writer creates stories. All writers do is catch and unearth stories.

According to King, stories are like fragile yet attractive shells, buried in the earth. The writer (or artist, or preacher for that matter) is just gifted with an eye to see the tip of the shell when no one else does. Once they have discovered the disturbance in the patter and the patternings of life, they painstakingly work at unearthing the shell, bit by bit, attempting not to crack it too much.

Leadership is all about the patter and the patternings. But few there are who teach how to listen to the patter, or look for the patternings. In fact, the nation's second director of national intelligence, Michael McConnell, sworn in on February 13, 2007, has admitted that "9/11 should have and could have been prevented" but the authorities simply "didn't connect the dots."[1]

To connect the dots, you must first discern the dots. Some people can't even see that there are dots (or shell-tips) to begin with.

Recently I conducted an advance in Africa on followership. Some of the best trackers of wild game in the world showed us how to play the game of "follow the leader"—read signs in nature and track "The Big Five." Simultaneously I reflected biblically and theologically on what it might mean for us to track the signs of the Spirit in the hunt for "Jesus sightings."

I confess that one of the biggest problems I had in learning how to track wild game in the African bush was that I didn't know the landscape well enough to know when it was "disturbed." Do we know the world of the Spirit well enough to detect disturbances in the wind, irruptions in the invisible?

You never know where God is going to unwind God's ladder.

OLD SAYING

The world is ruled by signs and signals. Signals are heavy-laden with social and moral connotations, and they alter the behavior of those receiving the signals.[2] In nature, you don't get to mate or even sometimes move without being able to read signs, many of them blazing signals in code: the crow of a rooster, the tail of a peacock, the antlers of a buck, the scent of an otter, the song of a kakapo.[3] In economics, the whole system of money is based on signs, and you can't balance a checkbook without the ability to read a sign language called "mathematics." You are tested in your sign-reading ability before you are given a license to drive a car.

Disciples of Jesus must learn to read the sign language of the Spirit. Sometimes God gives us a hint; sometimes God drops a hammer on us. But the handwriting is on the wall. God's finger is still writing. Can we read the signs of what God is doing? The ultimate in spiritual illiteracy is the inability to read the handwriting on the wall, especially when the essence of *euangelion* is announcing the good sign, the Jesus Sighting. Where Jesus is present, the possibility of miracles is also present.

MaryKate Morse has written a marvelous book which forces us to take a fresh look and a fresh listen at the visual and verbal markers we exchange on a daily basis. Almost overnight, there have appeared a host of "body language experts" vaunting their skills at reading nonverbal communication. But this is the first book in the religious world to look at the relationships between space, bodies and power, and to explore the nature of bodied influence. Where do you sit . . . in a room, at a table, at a lecture hall? How do you sit? When should you stand, and when should you sit?

Morse shows that when you say a person has "presence," it's not about what they say or do but their spirit, their ability to be in the moment. To read signals we need the arts of wonder, of intuition, of long-looking and hard-listening, of ethos and aesthetics. Morse most importantly draws back the curtains to reveal the smoke and mirrors behind the machines of "power" and the machinations of communication.

Maybe one day someone will establish a "sign school" for leaders. But until then, we have this book to instruct us in the techniques of sign-reading. You could profitably take an entire company or church staff through this Sign School, and each student would never see the world the same again.

At the conclusion of the debates that led to the signing of the United States Constitution, Benjamin Franklin spoke some words to those around him as colleagues were putting their own personal ink to the document. Franklin observed the patter and the patternings of the room they were in, especially a painting behind the president's chair that featured a vibrant sun. "I have," said he, "often and often, in the course of the session, and the vicissitudes of my hopes and fears as to its issue, looked at that behind the president, without being able to tell whether it was rising or setting; but now at length, I have the happiness to know, that it is a rising, and not a setting sun."[4]

The way to dream more vividly is to be wider awake to what is around you. Thank you, MaryKate Morse, for writing a book like none out there.

Leonard Sweet
Drew University, George Fox University

ACKNOWLEDGMENTS

I am deeply grateful for my husband, Randy, and my children, who encouraged me in the writing of this book. I'm thankful for many dear friends, especially Miriam Mendez, who supported me with their comments and companionship on this book-writing journey. I am also indebted to those who have experienced my leadership and learned with me while still loving me through the chaos of discovering how power happens in a group. My colleagues at the seminary of George Fox University gave helpful feedback and urged me on. The university also gave me release time to finish the manuscript—thank you. Many thanks go to my efficient research assistant, Lynn Landré, and to my daughter, Susanna, who carefully read and proofed the final draft. Finally, I am grateful to all those who told me their stories and brainstormed with me about power and influence. I am especially grateful to Kurt, my counselor, who influenced me to get off the bench and into the game. And this would not have been possible without the wisdom and skill of Cindy Bunch, my editor, and the helpfulness of the IVP staff. Thank you all.

INTRODUCTION

A Leadership Journey

Find a sandbox on a playground, and you'll find kids. A sandbox is a simple thing: a box with four sides, filled with sand. Kids don't need instructions on how to play in it. No training necessary. No classes. No nervous parents coaching from the sidelines. Children instinctively plunge in and create a miniature world of roads, bridges, castles, and moats. They create what they see and what they imagine. Sandboxes are a lot of fun. It's part of our DNA to make stuff out of raw material and to have fun with it. I think if no one were looking, we adults would get in and play too! But the fun stops when one child stakes claim to the sandbox and runs off the other kids. A discreet child might manage to stay, crouched in a corner playing quietly, but often it's not long before a carefully crafted tower gets stomped flat. Kids who rule sandboxes can do so because of their size and their "don't mess with me" attitude. Other kids steer clear, not wishing to risk bodily harm.

Life can be like a sandbox. Everyone is invited to play, but there's often someone charging around in the middle, knocking others out and stomping on the creativity of those in the corners. Why does this happen? Who says who gets to play and who doesn't? There seems to be some kind of cosmic sorting experience, like the Sorting Hat in the Harry Potter books. This hat, when placed on the heads of new students at Hogswarts School, would tell them into which house group they would go. Like the students with the Sorting Hat, it feels like we each sit with the hat placed on our head and hear, "You, go to the middle. Go crazy! Have fun!" Or, "You, off to the side. Be good and don't make any waves." It's like the hat knows. It's like we know. Even though we grow up, mature and gain experience, our bodies betray us. Our bodies carry the message of power. Our bodies tell others whether we have power (or not) and whether we will share it (or not).

This book is about unpacking the message our bodies send as we play together in the grown-ups' sandbox. It answers these questions: What is my body telling others? How can I become a player? If I'm already a player, how do I manage myself so that others are invited to play? As players, how do we use the group's power and resources to be Christ's light to a hurting world? This book is for anyone who wants to make a difference yet knows that *wanting* and *making* are two very different things. This book is especially geared toward leaders and potential leaders, for those who mentor and guide them, and for groups who want to lead together.

The foundational premise is this: Power is constituted between persons in a group through myriads of little body cues and instinctual decisions. Power, which gives an individual or a group the right to influence, is created through the small decisions groups make about who will be entrusted with the leadership baton and who will not. Leaders are not simply born or made. Leadership is an intricate dance between potential leaders and their followers so that power is group-made. Everyone reads the unspoken language of the body. People don't just take up the space needed to become leaders; others give them that space. Either they need that person to be their leader;

or they are too afraid to challenge the abuse of power; or they themselves are powerless, and no one listens to their voice.

God created us to have a meaningful life, and leaders especially yearn to make a difference. Life is rich, chaotic, and sometimes dark, but everyone deserves to play in the sandbox, even to be in the center occasionally. By the time you finish this book, you will understand yourself and your sandbox better. You will understand your own power and how to use it well, without chasing anyone away or retreating into the shadows. And you will learn practical ways to experience satisfaction in the ministry of making a difference.

I wrote this book out of my love of being in the game and influencing others, and out of my own personal experience of learning how to play well with others. It took me several years to learn how to live out my calling in the sandbox. It took even more time to figure out how to be a healthy individual and a Christlike influencer of others.

The seed for this book grew out of a phrase that my counselor, Kurt, often repeated to me: "There is no free space. Get out of the corner, into the game, and play." At that time I was struggling with how to make a difference. As a Christian called to lead, I wanted to contribute to making the world a better place, but I had trouble understanding the difference between carrying in my body the image of Christ as servant and as Lord. When I felt powerless, I wondered if that was how to be a servant. Then when I felt powerful, I struggled with the impact I had on playing the game and whether or not that impact was Christlike.

I couldn't find the balance between being myself while holding Christ at the center and taking up space to accomplish God's purposes. I found that others felt the same way. I was frustrated with other leaders who seemed oblivious to how they used their bodies to assert power plays during meetings. They would take up lots of space, and the rest of the group would be squashed against the sides of the sandbox. I was frustrated with myself and church elders and prominent Christian leaders who couldn't figure out how to help leaders do better with their power. So I began a journey, a leadership journey to understand power. The biblical story that captures the whole of this journey is Luke 7:36-50, the story of Jesus and a sinful woman in the house of Simon the Pharisee. This story taught me about Jesus' use of power, Jesus' leadership, and how power used well can make a big difference in someone's life. The story also taught me about the destructiveness of power used poorly, even for holy reasons, and the potential for the powerless to have an important moral voice.

On my journey to understand power, I tried different leadership approaches: directive, nondirective, lay-centered, servant, empowering, transformational, emotionally intelligent—and all the while, I kept running into the complexity of being me in a group with other persons. It became clear that it wasn't just about me figuring myself out. It was about what happens when a group interacts around topics that matter to the individuals or the collective whole. Individuals bring their own stuff, which they carry in their bodies, to the sandbox. The group creates new stuff in the sandbox. In the end, some are given power and others are not. And it all happens instinctually.

I have been a leader, and I have been involved with leaders, in churches, denominations, academic institutions, and parachurch and mission organizations for more than thirty years. Along the way I've picked up haphazard clues about leadership. I've observed both the positives and negatives of power within groups. I've had hundreds of conversations about power with people in Christian organizations, and each time I learn more. Everyone has a story about their own experiences with power and powerlessness. Many leaders have felt the same frustration in trying to interpret what happens with power in the sandbox. I share several of those true stories in this book, though I've changed some details to protect the privacy of the sources. In those cases where a story is told without changes, I've obtained permission from the teller.

In addition to gathering stories, I also did research. I read about leadership, organizational systems, Jesus and New Testament studies, gender and race issues, psychology and the social sciences. This part of the journey was not entirely systematic; I felt as if I were solving a nonlinear mystery that took many divergent paths along the way. I stumbled upon Edward Hall's research and became intrigued by the relationship of the use of physical space to our identities and group interactions.[1] Hall explains that power involves a social physicality, a body-to-body conversation. When I studied social science research on Jesus, I came across information on the first-century economic system and the impact Jesus had on it. I discovered that Jesus taught and lived an economy of hospitality while Western economy today is one of consumerism. I found that power can be used in social settings either to consume or invite. For example, there is a monumental contrast between the way Bill Clinton used his body to abuse his presidential power with Monica Lewinsky and the way Rosa Parks used her body in a symbolic action that was born out of her powerlessness.

We don't talk about this much. Over and over again, powerful people compromise or severely weaken organizations because of their poor choices. Megachurch pastor Ted Haggard, isolated in his paradoxical world of invincibility as God's man for the times, was at the same time making small, dark and destructive choices. And then he fell from influence. How does something like that happen to a "moral" leader? It's too simple of an answer to say Ted Haggard sinned. Who mentored him or counseled him about the intoxicating, blinding effect of fame? Any man or woman can make mistakes when a group keeps them isolated in the center of the sandbox. This pedestal-placing disconnects the leaders' bodies from others who have the potential to help them play well.

This book provides a way to see and manage how we carry the power of our bodies in the sandbox. My hope is that this book will catalyze conversations about power and its stewardship, and that today's leaders will create and work together better so we can live out Christ's purposes in the world. That hope will only be realized when we can name what we know about power, have safe ways to talk about it, and then manage it well.

1

BODIED INFLUENCE

Leadership and the Body

The privilege of mattering
is what is at stake here.
VANESSA OCHS

> To all who received him, who believed
> in his name, he gave power to become
> children of God.
> JOHN 1:12

BEN'S STORY

Several years ago Ben, a young representative on a senior-level board of a Christian organization, attended a typical board meeting. Usually board meetings fade quickly from memory, but Ben found himself thinking about this one over and over. It troubled him. It wasn't the content of the meeting that bothered him, but a seemingly insignificant development that he'd noticed between the lines. The meeting had been specially called, and Ben was pleased with the creative problem-solving the group applied to a particularly thorny issue. They spent a couple of hours in discussion before coming to a solution. Everyone in the group contributed, and they felt good about the decision.

But during a coffee break, the scene changed. A popular local pastor rushed into the room, apologizing for being held up in another meeting. What caught Ben's attention was not the pastor or his lateness, but the reaction of the other board members. Everyone rose to greet him, extending hands and making room for him to join the group. The energy in the room lifted. Several people began talking at the same time. As soon as the pastor was seated, a couple individuals summarized the discussion up to that point and then asked for his opinion. Everyone was watching him. The pastor launched into a small presentation on how he saw the issue, which was very different from the conclusion Ben and the others had drawn earlier. The group began talking again and in the end changed their decision to correspond to the views of the come-late pastor. The meeting again came to a close for a refreshment break.

Ben was astonished. What had just happened? Hadn't they all worked carefully and thoughtfully on the issue for some time? Didn't the conclusions of the first discussion count for something? How did this pastor have the influence to create such a tizzy in a roomful of experienced and sober-minded leaders?

The pastor remained seated at the meeting table looking through some papers, so Ben approached him and said, "Wow! That was something. Did you see what just happened here?"

"What?" he responded.

"Well, everyone turned to you, and we changed our decision after you spoke!"

The pastor said nothing, so Ben pressed on. "Excuse me, sir, I'm interested in how you handle that kind of power. How do you manage it so it doesn't corrupt your soul?"

The pastor just looked at Ben, got up and walked away. From then on, whenever the two of them were in the same social setting, Ben was ignored.

MY STORY

Like Ben, I've been pushed to the corner of the sandbox. Some time ago I ran into an eminent individual, an elderly statesman widely known in a certain circle for his leadership roles and his strong presence. He was not a tall man, but when he spoke, his voice boomed as if he were speaking to a crowd in a stadium. I saw him in a hallway as we were going in different directions. Wanting to be friendly, I initiated a conversation. "Hi! I see we're speakers at the same conference coming up."

He stopped right in front of me, leaned in close and carefully said, "I am the speaker. You are a workshop presenter." With that, he walked away.

Why did he invade my space like that? Why did he need to assert his position over me? I felt like a scraggly hen in the chicken coop who'd just been booted out by the chief rooster.

Both the popular pastor and the elderly statesmen were leaders. Both exercised their influence in two minor encounters. But these little things tell a big story. Leadership is not something produced for certain occasions and specific roles. Leadership happens all the time, and it happens when we use our bodies to influence others.

THE PHYSICAL NATURE OF LEADERSHIP

The terms *leader* and *leadership* are relatively new to the English language, coming into use only in the last few hundred years.[1] Prior to that, role titles such as *priest, king* and *captain* conferred authority and power. Leadership came out of one's role in a social system. A person who had a position of authority was the leader—it was as simple as that. So using the term *leader* was unnecessary, and further thought about the concept of leadership was irrelevant. Today, however, the topic is more complicated, and it is widely discussed. Understanding leaders and leadership is a major money-making business, from books to seminars, from studies to consultants, from training centers to degree-conferring institutions. Yet what is it, really?

Today's basic definition is this: leadership means influence. Leaders influence others more than they are influenced themselves. The pastor and the statesman both exerted their influence—one on the board members, the other on me. One changed the outcome of a board's hard-earned decision. The other tried to change the direction of my thoughts. Most people understand that leadership has a moral component, but it isn't easy to unpack the moral ramifications of subtle moments of influence such as these. Did these two leaders do something "wrong" in the way they used their influence? If so, how is it talked about?

Leadership is a mysterious and complex relational process between a leader (or leaders) and a group so that everyone pursues a redemptive present and a transformational future. We often reduce leadership to vision statements, strategic plans, communiqués, budgets, even character traits for building and sustaining trust, and emotional savvy for handling conflict. Sometimes we reduce leadership to a person's role or title. This extreme simplification is the most deceptive of all. If we call someone a leader or make them a leader, does it guarantee that leadership will happen? Sometimes. But leadership is more complex than role-titling. We also oversimplify the nature of leadership by reducing it to a slogan. For example, "You can tell if you're a leader because there are followers behind you." But maybe those followers simply want to be paid, or you're the only leader they have. Having followers doesn't necessarily mean that authentic leadership is happening.

Though titles, followers, vision statements and goals may be markers of leadership, true leadership happens between the lines, in the interpersonal relational processes in social settings. This is a different way of looking at it. Effective leadership is traditionally measured by character traits or outcomes such as employee satisfaction or growth. This often leads churches and businesses to focus on the scoreboard rather than on how the game is played. The game is won by the hundreds of small decisions and interactions among the players, which indicate whether they are playing as a team or as individuals. If you want to understand how to win the game, you have to understand the nuances of how the game is played between the players.

Leadership is a physical and social process. It is thousands of little body postures, gestures, nuanced voices and intricate, intuitive engagements with others. It is how you enter a room, position yourself to speak, modulate your voice and use your eyes, while at the same time assessing others who are sharing that same space. It is an assessment of the power quotient of each person in the group. Leadership involves stewardship of one's own physical being and the physical being of others. When we acknowledge this, we can begin to observe, talk about and manage the power resources of each person in our group.

The pastor in Ben's story took up a great deal of social space, and the others in the boardroom gave it to him without question. He had certain personal credentials: education, explosive success, articulate and engaging speaking abilities, social skills, and good looks. The pastor's rise to popularity was meteoric. Unfortunately, the fame and hype gradually slipped away as he struggled with relational problems in his church. But for a period of time, he exercised enormous influence. He was the golden boy—but not because he gave himself that title. His church and his denomination needed him to be successful. If he was successful, they were too. They could declare that their Christian organization was going somewhere because they had a bright leader to help them succeed.

The elderly statesman I met in the hall also took up space. Even though he was a small man, he had learned to make himself seem bigger by projecting his voice. He had learned to use his body posture to assert authority. Others were comfortable with his style because it created a sense of security among them. Both of these leaders had power given to them by others, and both of them carried that confidence in their bodies.

I believe this is one of the reasons that Jesus came in the flesh. Perhaps it would have been easier for us if Jesus had come as a powerful spiritual being; an invincible angel-god would have gotten the world's attention rather nicely. But Jesus did not simply come to make a point; he came to transform us. Jesus lived out for us how our very being, our very body, though finite, has the potential to influence others toward love and blessing. Philippians 2 reminds us that Jesus took on the form of a servant and became human in likeness and form.

Josephus, a first-century Jewish historian, wrote that Jesus was a person of no special appearance. It was humbling enough for him to take on the form of a human being, even more so to be a rather ordinary one. That should encourage those of us who see ourselves as ordinary in appearance. Jesus was a minimalist. He pared himself down as much as possible so that we could identify with him, his mission and his capacity to love despite the spite and hate he received. He modeled leadership as a powerful thing in a human body that cares about the great concerns of God's kingdom. Jesus came in the flesh to influence us toward a living picture of God's kingdom. We can follow in his footsteps by taking our ordinary form and, along with others, blessing a blighted world. But how do we do that? In our best moments, we all want to do that. I am fairly certain that the pastor and the statesman really cared about God's kingdom, really wanted to lead as Jesus led. I'm sure they wanted to make a difference as Christian leaders, but something slipped them up along the way.

So where do we as leaders begin in understanding, changing and managing the use of our bodies in relational space? We start with Jesus, the master influencer. We start with a brief review of what the kingdom is, how Jesus is the head of the kingdom, and what the believing body has to do with it.

THE KINGDOM: MAKING A DIFFERENCE IN A PHYSICAL WORLD

Stories about kings and queens, quests and adventures, usually hold a lot of appeal for children, both boys and girls. When I was a little girl, stories about princesses and knights and love and honor were exciting to me. I could imagine that I, too, was strong and courageous and able to do the right thing. When my life was in a dark place, I would escape into a fairy-tale world where everything worked out and people were loved and treated well. But as an adult, I found the real-life world to be less noble. Things were more complex, and there were few simple solutions. I was more broken than I realized, and so was everyone else. When I chose to follow Jesus in college, I found that I belonged to a kingdom with a great leader who is righteous and merciful and fair and very real to me. But since then I've also found that this kingdom is still sometimes ambiguous and tangled and requires careful understanding of its nature.

The kingdom of God, sometimes called the kingdom of heaven, is a primary theme in Scripture. In the Old Testament, God's kingdom is pictured as an everlasting and glorious kingdom that has dominion and authority over all creation. God's kingdom encompasses all of heaven and earth, and it can never be destroyed. It is holy, just and righteous. God is the one who establishes, sets up, tears down, builds and plants the kingdoms of the world. God declared that earthly kingdoms endure when they are holy. Israel was to be a priestly kingdom and a holy nation, set apart to reflect God's holiness and to bless all other nations.

In the New Testament, the term *kingdom* is used 128 times in the Gospels alone. Of those, 93 are instances where Jesus himself used the phrase "kingdom of God" or "kingdom of heaven." Jesus said that he came to proclaim the kingdom, and the kingdom was near. He came to seek and save the lost, all types of lost—economically, morally, relationally and spiritually. Jesus did not equate the kingdom with the power of royalty but with the power of a community of redeemed persons. His kingdom power has to do with a love for all people and a desire to bring them under the protection and redemptive power of God's wing. Jesus commissions his followers to follow—to do what he did, how he did it. Through the proclamation, teaching and healing of Jesus and his followers together, the rule of God's kingdom happens. We do not create or introduce the kingdom. The kingdom of God is within and all around his followers, who join together to incarnate the image of God through Jesus Christ. That is the power of God's kingdom, which has power over all other authorities and dominions and self-serving rulers because the power of God's kingdom is internal and eternal. It cannot be overcome.

Jesus rarely spoke about being born again. Only in the Gospel of John did he speak about being "born from above" (often translated as "born again") or born of "water" and "Spirit." The rebirth of individuals was only a part of Jesus' wider vision to restore God's kingdom of love and justice by calling his followers to influence the world for his kingdom. Jesus proclaimed a kingdom that is set within all people and is marked by a righteousness of love rather than law-keeping. People become God's children through a relationship of grace rather than mere affiliation. Every follower becomes a royal priest, committed to interceding on behalf of, blessing and loving all other humans in the world. In the strictest sense, none of us is really a leader or a pastor or a priest or a bishop. We all have one authority, and we've all been given the influence to seek and enter into the kingdom of God as servants of Christ. Not all of us have been given the gift of leadership, but all of us do have the responsibility to make sure leadership happens the way Jesus modeled it.

THE KING: JESUS LEADING THE WAY AS A SERVANT

A kingdom is a monarchy. Even though Jesus often spoke about the kingdom of God, he did not use language describing himself as King. Instead, Jesus talked about the least being the greatest, about humbling ourselves and serving each other. He talked about being a servant to his disciples, and he demonstrated it by washing their feet and giving his life for them. Yet Jesus also spoke with authority and clarity. He did not shirk from calling a spade a spade, such as when he called the Pharisees "whitewashed tombs." He was not afraid to upset the established religious system by throwing out of the temple the money changers who regularly cheated the poor. Huge crowds followed him, and important personages sought an audience with him. He was a teacher, a sage, a servant, even a miracle worker. Trained religious leaders felt threatened by his prophetic and healing ministry. Although Jesus had a tremendous amount of power, he did not refer to himself as a leader or a king. Yet no one else has influenced this world as much as Jesus.

In the Gospels, only Luke 1:33 records this announcement: "He will reign over the house of Jacob for ever, and of his kingdom there will be no end." After Jesus' birth, wise men from the East came seeking a king of the Jews. John's Gospel records that Nathanael called Jesus "the King of Israel" the first time he met Jesus. Jesus told several parables about kings. And during his triumphant entry into Jerusalem at the beginning of the Passover, all the Gospels record how the crowd proclaimed the coming of the King. Yet when the crowd wanted to make him a king, Jesus quietly withdrew. During Jesus' trial, Pilate asked him if he was the King of the Jews, and he responded, "You say so." Then he was mocked as a king, and over his head Pilate gave notice of his fatal offense: "This is Jesus, the King of the Jews." So the language of "king" is used at Jesus' birth and his trial and death; but during his ministry, Jesus did not refer to his authority or power in those terms.

This is how Jesus talks about his relationship with his disciples during his last meal with them: he took bread and broke it and said, "Take, eat; this is my body" (Mt 26:26). Then he took wine and told them, "Drink from it, all of you; for this is my blood of the covenant, which is poured out for many for the forgiveness of sins" (Mt 26:27-28). In other words, Jesus gives all that he is—his very body and blood—for the sake of God's kingdom purposes. And God's purpose is that all people might know the fullness of Jesus incarnated in each of his followers. This is multiplied influence! This is why Jesus said that we would do greater works than he. Jesus did not give us a slogan to follow or a strategic plan but his very body given completely for us. The King of the kingdom is identified not by a golden crown or flowing robes or an elegant throne, but by an ordinary-looking body, broken for our wholeness.

Paul, the first great missionary of the church, took Jesus' language about his body and used it to talk about Jesus as the head of his body the church. The church is the living body of Christ. We are many members of one common, incarnate presence. The source of the church's authority and power is the head—in Greek, the *kephale*—of the body. The word *kephale* is rich in meaning and grounded in organic reality. *Kephale* can be defined either as the source of a stream or the head of a body. It can also refer to a scout who goes before an army to spy on the enemy. Thus, *kephale* communicates the ideas of safety, source and intelligence. Since only one head is connected to the body, the only true leader is Christ. Our primary responsibility as members and followers is to remain attached to the head. Since the body is experienced through its senses, our attachment to Christ is not a spiritual, out-of-body experience. Coming to know the mind and heart of Christ happens through our bodies—through our nervous system, our brains, the beating of our hearts, the touch, smell, and sight of life around us. In this world, our spiritual attachments are temporarily housed in finite bodies that are constantly relating to other bodies.

THE SUBJECTS: CALLED TO MAKE A DIFFERENCE

If Jesus is the head of the body, then it follows that we are the members of the body. As Paul says in his writings, we are linked together in a permanent, unbreakable way. A body does not cut off its parts or rearrange its members. Systems theory teaches about the connectedness of all life, but first-century Jews already understood the foundational nature of our connectedness. Paul writes that we are many members, that we are joined and knit together and all drink of same Spirit. The result is the natural growth of God's kingdom and the building up of the body in love. This vision of the body included Jews and Greeks, slaves and free, male and female, the barbarian and the cultured. There are no parts that are specially blessed or more necessary than others. There are no parts that can function on their own, apart from other brothers and sisters in Christ. This has profound implications for leaders and leadership in the church.

The church as the body of Christ and Christ as the head of the body has been written about, preached about and talked about for centuries. But most communities of believers—churches, parachurch or other Christian organizations—do not know how to trust the leading of Christ among us. Part of that is because we do not understand how to discern together his leading. Part of it is because we abdicate leadership responsibility to persons in traditional leadership roles or to persons who take up a lot of space in our meetings and other interactions. To recapture the true functioning of the kingdom of God, all members of the body must revive their investment in the health of the church and the concerns of God's kingdom in the world.

As one physical whole, we all have a responsibility to pay attention to our own influence. If we are to function fully as the body of Christ, we can't have the majority acting as hands and feet while only a few make decisions and influence the church. Surely as head of the church Jesus intended that all members of his body would listen for his divine will and attend to his holy purposes in whichever community of believers we belong to. Perhaps we fear that if everyone has responsibility and everyone has a voice, there will be anarchy and rebellions and divisions popping up like fireworks on the Fourth of July—lots of sparks and gasps of awe, but no cohesive power to move forward in a God-honoring way.

The fear is legitimate. Divisions do happen both in small and large organizations. It's not that leaders, pastors, elders and committee chairs are not important—the body does have separate parts. But Jesus envisioned a body functioning together as the kingdom of God. In order to work together, to be truly linked by ligaments and sinews, each member of the body must see himself or herself as an influencing member. Each of us has a responsibility to be influencers in God's kingdom, whether we belong to a church of fifty members in rural Iowa or a church of five thousand in downtown New York. Leadership isn't abdicated but joined.

BODIED INFLUENCE

Jesus came in the flesh to influence us toward a living picture of God's true kingdom. Jesus described himself as the head of the body, the church. This organic image encourages us to perceive the church and Jesus' leadership of it through the senses. Leadership among Christians involves both a physical and a group dynamic: it has a physical dynamic because people instinctively use their bodies to influence others by taking up space in social settings. It has a group dynamic because each person's presence and role contribute to influencing the group toward spiritual, cognitive and relational wholeness.

Authentic leadership—leadership that catalyzes a group toward deep change and moves its members in positive, energizing directions—involves the group acting together. A leader helps give form and direction, but everyone, regardless of gender, age or amount of experience, has the right and responsibility to be part of the influencing process. Therefore, if things are going well, the leader and the group celebrate together. Success is not seen as the result of one person's accomplishments. The leader knows he or she could not accomplish much without the group. If things are not going well, the leader and the group figure out why. Failure is not seen as the leader's sole responsibility. Problems can rarely be reduced to a single cause that can be blamed on one person. The movement of the body toward the kingdom of God with Christ as our head requires each member to take an active role in the leadership process.

Bodied influence is communal and is observed both spiritually and physically. With Christ as the head, the reality of Christlikeness is experienced throughout the body, creating energy, joy and health in the body. Such a picture of health is compelling to a culture hungry for love, purpose, community and spiritual connection.

QUESTIONS FOR DISCUSSION

1. Share your own story of an encounter with a person of power that left you feeling dismissed or confused. Why do you think the pastor and the statesman described in this chapter acted as they did?

2. All of us have used our bodies to assert our authority over someone else. In what ways have you done this?

3. What does it mean for your church or organization to be the kingdom of God? How might you think about your values and plans as an element of God's kingdom rather than as part of a denomination, a parachurch organization or a local church?

4. How could a group structure itself so that Christ is the true head? How would you differentiate between personal agendas and the influence of Christ?

5. How does being a member of the body of Christ affect the way you think about your role in a group? What role should the leaders have, and what role should others have?

2

HOLDING THE DYNAMITE

The Ethics of Power

**With great power comes
great responsibility.**
UNCLE BEN IN *SPIDER-MAN*

**For God did not give us a spirit of
cowardice, but rather a spirit of power
and of love and of self-discipline.**
2 TIMOTHY 1:7

MARK'S STORY

Mark, a youth pastor at a large suburban church, sat in a meeting of
the church's search committee for hiring a senior pastor. They had
interviewed several individuals and were preparing to make a final
decision. Everyone except Mark and the church secretary, Bess, fa-
vored hiring Jim, who came highly recommended by denominational
leaders. However, during the interview process, Jim had said he only
wanted to preach and counsel people one-on-one in his office. He

did not like meetings or working with other staff members—he did not feel that was his role. Mark wondered if Jim was only comfortable in situations where he had full control and authority, such as the pulpit and the pastoral counseling office. Mark thought it was important for a senior pastor to be relationally astute in all types of situations. Bess was uncomfortable with Jim because she knew she would need to have a good relationship with him as his secretary, and she felt that Jim had ignored her and her questions during the interview process. During the committee's discussion, Mark and Bess were routinely ignored whenever they raised an objection or asked for clarification concerning the selection of Jim.

"It was like I wasn't even there," Mark explained to me later. "And sure enough, after Jim came, things went from bad to worse. Bess eventually quit—the best church secretary we ever had. Jim treated her like a doormat and expected her to immediately comply with his every demand. He constantly questioned her competency. Jim told me I wasn't the kind of youth pastor he was looking for, then he fired me and hired his nephew, who didn't have any training or experience! Because of his imperious style, people started drifting away from the church, and Jim didn't seem to care. When the church's numbers went from 700 to 230 and the tithing income dropped to a fraction of its previous levels, the elders finally let him go—with a hefty severance package, of course. Why hadn't they listened to Bess and me?" Mark asked a great question. Why were Mark and Bess ignored during this important decision? Why were they powerless to stop the committee from hiring Jim?

EILEEN'S STORY

Eileen was one of the most fragile human beings I have ever met. She shivered as she sat across from me in my office, reminding me of a cracked window pane—any careless gesture or word might cause her to shatter into pieces. With her small frame hunkered down, she told me in halting whispers of a long string of profound injustices in her life. She began with her wealthy, reputable and church-elder husband, who had battered her physically and verbally in the secret of their home. He called her incompetent, pathetic and unworthy as a wife and mother. Because she loved her four children so much, and because she believed she was to love her husband no matter what, she continued in the marriage. She had gone to the pastor of her church for help, and he told her that if she fully submitted to her husband's authority, he would be a good husband. If she was kinder and more loving, he wouldn't get angry. After fourteen years, her husband filed for divorce, saying she had cheated on him and was mentally incompetent. No one believed her side of the story, and even her lawyer did not defend her. She lost her home and her children and was left with no financial support.

Eileen moved to another state, where she found a position as an administrative assistant in her denomination's hospital. One of the hospital's staff leaders began stalking her. When she reported it, the leadership told her she was tempting this man with her beauty and provocative dress, though she complied with the hospital's dress code and wore long skirts and shirts that covered her arms and neck. Eventually the man trapped her in an isolated part of the building and raped her. Eileen quit her job and moved to another part of town. I met her soon after that. Somewhere in the midst of her pain, Eileen felt that God still loved her and had called her to help others. But she could hardly lift her head up. How had Eileen been stripped of her voice and her power? Why hadn't others believed her and helped her?

CONFUSION ABOUT POWER

When I ask people to tell me about a time when they felt powerless, and to describe what that powerlessness felt like, they usually say they felt helpless, vulnerable and small, out of control, frightened, unloved, anxious. No one talks about powerlessness as a positive experience. On the other hand, when I ask them to tell of a time when they felt powerful, they talk about feeling excited, energized, hopeful, fulfilled, responsible, and then cautious as they recognized the emotional headiness of power and its ability to destabilize them.

Feeling powerful is a wonderful sensation. But many Christians have a love-hate relationship with the word *power*. Christians love having God's power, but we shun the use of human power. We tend to think that human power is always corrupt while God's power is always pure. We know that power struggles in churches and Christian organizations often lead to open conflicts or silent misunderstandings that can simmer for years. Different interpretations of God's will can erect impenetrable walls between believers. Humans can abuse power, and when they do, those in the margins suffer. Power corrupts office holders, business leaders, athletes and pastors. So the age-old story goes.

On the other hand, we know that when God's power is unleashed, the heavens are opened and souls are saved. God's power created the heavens and the earth. God's power opened up the Red Sea, held back the sun and caused the big fish to swallow Jonah and then spit him up on the beach. Jesus Christ is the "power of God" (1 Cor 1:24). Jesus demonstrated his power through miracles and wonders, creating a following of those hungry for renewal for themselves and for Israel. Jesus multiplied bread, healed lepers, raised people from the dead and upended tables in the temple of God. Jesus promised his followers that they would do even greater works. The Holy Spirit was poured out on a small band of Jesus' followers, giving them the capacity to continue Christ's wonders and miracles. Today the Holy Spirit gives us power to accomplish God's purposes. Therefore, holy power is God's power.

On the other hand, Jesus also calls us to be servants, not power brokers. God is the one who sets people in authority. Like Jesus, we should submit to those in authority. So we tend to associate all "good" power with God's sovereign will and all "bad" power with human endeavors. We can probably all agree that God's power through the Holy Spirit is holy power. But does that mean human power is always bad? Does it mean God's power and human power are always two separate things?

The people in power are often the most ignorant about the negative emotional impact that powerlessness has on those deprived of voice and value. This is clearly apparent with the issue of race in the United States. We have made a tremendous amount of progress since my college years in Prince Edward County, Virginia, in the seventies. My freshman class had the first African American student ever to be admitted to the all female school. I and others invited this young woman to attend a popular local church that had a progressive and dynamic pastor. She attended one Sunday morning, and the next day she was called into the school president's office, where she faced a group of white male elders telling her she couldn't come back to that church. "We can't worship with you present," they said. "It's distracting."

We might be horrified by this story, but things like this still happen today. Black males suffer police profiling. Asian females are ignored. Mexican Americans are verbally harassed for taking American jobs. An Asian leader in InterVarsity Christian Fellowship told me that sometimes after speaking engagements people have said to him, "Go home, Chinaman." Powerlessness is a nasty, ugly business. Only those who have personally experienced the force of it really understand that it cannot be romanticized as service or humility. Power is a gift from God. Power used well is healing. Power used poorly is sinful. Powerlessness is not a state of grace but of sin.

Those with power often speak for those without. But they cannot possibly describe, define or rationalize the impact of powerlessness on the human spirit because they don't know it. I have ministered for twenty-two years in theological education, an environment dominated by males. After several years of working with one dean, he told me, "I never really understood how much of a glass ceiling there is for women or the extra obstacles they have to overcome. I'm ashamed to say that I thought women exaggerated those problems. I know now I was wrong. It's tough for women."

In the stories in this chapter, Mark, Bess and Eileen all felt powerless. They were unable to influence their situations. Those with power abused it. As a result, things happened that should not happen in God's kingdom. What would have happened if Eileen and Mark and Bess had been more powerful? If they'd had a sense of personal power, would things have gone differently?

We often make the mistake of assuming that all power is bad because we've seen it used badly by imperfect human beings. We come to the conclusion that power corrupts and is contrary to "servant leadership."[1] So we avoid talking about power at all. We fail to ask the important questions, who has it? Who doesn't? And how is it being used? We think that labeling Christian leaders as "servant leaders" resolves the issue so that we don't need to talk about power. But things not talked about are things ignored. And things ignored eventually come up for air.

RICK'S STORY

Rick came from a privileged family life, where getting the best education, taking European vacations and receiving expensive gifts, like a Harley Davidson, were normal. He was a leader from grade school on, and he thrived as one. His family wanted him to follow in his dad's footsteps and become a partner in the family law firm. But in college, Rick felt called to the ministry, and he chose to go to seminary in Kentucky rather than law school. When he returned to Atlanta trained, ordained and supported by his denomination, Rick began planting a church in a blue-collar part of town. Even though

Rick was doing well as a pastor, he struggled with guilt over the privileges he'd received in his life. So Rick bent over backwards to serve. He listened carefully to others. He got involved in the city's homeless shelter services. He moved into a neighborhood that matched the status of his church members. Still he felt it wasn't enough. Power was always given to him. Success always came. It made Rick feel uneasy and insecure. Was this power from God? Should he give it up? How should he use it?

These are all important questions. If we are to be God's influencers, we need to come to grips with the true role of power in our lives. If we are to incarnate the living presence of Christ, we must understand the combination of his power with our own. When we hold the dynamite, we need to know whether we are using it for God's purposes or for selfish ends. This is not always easy to sort out, as Rick well knew.

POWER IS ESSENTIAL FOR LIFE

Power is less like a tool we use to make something happen and more like the water we drink to stay alive. Personal power is essential. It means knowing that I am an individual and can make decisions about my life. Personal power is key to emotional health and well-being. If we don't have a sense of personal power, we will struggle. In his classic book *Power and Innocence,* Rollo May writes, "Power and the sense of significance . . . are intertwined."[2] Power is a basic part of our DNA. Personal power leads to the freedom to exercise power in relationships with others. Eileen, the emotionally battered wife, did not have a sense of personal power. Without a sense of significance, she was unable to go outside her denominational circle and ask for help. She could not go to the police or find a lawyer who believed her. She couldn't see that what was happening to her was a gross offense to God. She couldn't imagine that anyone would believe her.

Power is simply the "ability to cause or prevent change."[3] The difference between God's power and human power is a matter of scale, not necessarily quality. Therefore, human beings can use power in the same way Jesus did. In healthy settings, individuals have the power to make changes in their lives, either internally or externally. They are free to contribute to the well-being of their community. Mark and Bess, though apparently seen as less significant members of the search committee, still had the right to express their views in the decision-making process. This essential ability to choose does not come with one's name on an office door or with a specific role. It is the nature of being human. Rick's personal power was a good thing, not something to feel guilty about. The confidence and opportunities that came with it were allowing him to make a difference in his community. However, personal power does come with risk, and it happens in community.

GOD CREATED HUMANITY TO EXERCISE POWER

From the biblical story of creation we get two important concepts. First, God created human beings to reflect God's image: "God said, 'Let us make humankind in our image, according to our likeness.' . . . God created humankind in his own image, in the image of God he created them; male and female he created them" (Gen 1:26-27). Our ability to make decisions, respond to others, care about beauty and kindness, and do important work is part of God's nature that is imprinted on us. We are designed to have power. Second, we are to subdue the earth and have dominion over every living thing. Twice God says "let them have dominion over." "Dominion," *urdu*, a Hebrew word, means "rule" or "dominion." God created men and women to have authority, and after blessing Adam and Eve he commands them to exercise it. Therefore, it was and is God's intention that people have the power to steward and nurture the earth and its resources. The intent is not to lord it over others or use other people and resources for personal gain, but to manage it wisely, as farmers manage their animals or fields.

THE EXERCISE OF POWER HAS MORAL IMPLICATIONS

Power is essential, and authority is given to us by God. It begins with a sense of personal empowerment. As babies and toddlers, a loving and valuing home environment breeds a capacity for personal power. Those internal experiences of personal power are invariably expressed with others in social settings. Power exchanged, given or earned in those settings is called social power. The way social power is expressed varies significantly. Though power itself is neutral, how we use it is not. Power can be used for good or for bad. Power can water a garden or flood a valley. The ability to cause or prevent change can either benefit others or simply oneself.

To understand the moral implications of power, it helps to have a framework for the various kinds of power exercised in interpersonal relationships. I've adapted the four categories developed by social psychologists French and Raven in their classic study on power.[4] The four categories are *expert, character, role* and *culture*. The descriptions of how each social power is used for positive or negative effects are my own.

Expert power accrues to someone who has special knowledge, skills, training or significant experience. Expert power can be earned or gained. The higher the educational degree, the more specialized the knowledge or skill, the more years of proven success and experience, the more expert power a person is given. In the church, the pastor known for the gift of preaching, the financial adviser chairing the stewardship committee, or the worship leader with amazing talent on the piano are given more status and opportunity because of their expertise. In the academic world, the professor known as an expert in a particular field of study gains this type of power. Even a group can earn it. A church that has grown to thousands of members, a grant organization that has raised millions of dollars, a ministry that is effectively helping people overcome addictions— these groups often serve as guides to others. They might sponsor conferences, train leaders or act as consultants.

Character power endows a person with special status and voice because of the observed quality of their character. Character power is given to a person by a group—an individual cannot claim it for himself or herself. This bestowed power recognizes the person's honesty, morality and integrity. The group can expect that this person will do the right thing. In most Christian faith communities, a person who follows a Christian code of ethics, worships regularly and tithes, and volunteers in the church and the community is given character power. These qualities indicate a special kind of devotion to God and holiness. In some faith communities, the exercise of charismatic gifts also indicates holiness and God's special favor. Those who display such gifts are given more character power.

Role power is given to those who serve a particular role in an organization. They have a job to fulfill. They are given the authority to reward, such as raising a person's salary, or to punish, such as firing someone. Role power is positional authority. The boss at work, the governor of the state, parents at home or a pastor in a church have power because of their role. With this type of power, a person can reward or coerce or punish others because of his or her position of authority over them. Like expert power, role power can be given to individuals or groups. In some Christian organizations, for instance, board members are given the power to make major decisions, but in others, the group as a whole has that power.

Culture power varies from culture to culture and depends on who and what each culture values more. Those that are valued are given more power to influence. Since this book is written by a Westerner in the United States, the cultural descriptors reflect what Westerners value. The culture values of an Asian person from Korea or a Latino from Mexico would be different. But whatever the culture values, to that it will give an extra measure of power. For example, we in the United States give athletes and actors a great deal of status. We pay them enormous amounts of money. We seem to care about every detail of their lives. We listen to their opinions on topics. We allow them to influence us because we value their accomplishments. In the church, we give culture power to pastors of the biggest churches because we often equate membership numbers with success.

All four types of power can be used either for good or for bad. Each can be exercised in ways that benefit and help others or that enhance the status, wealth or influence of the individual or group wielding the power. People who share their expertise and train others use expert power in a positive way. Knowledge is shared, and the next generation is mentored. On the other hand, people who hoard knowledge and use it to protect personal interests use expert power in a negative way. They can withhold information in order to get the outcome they desire. Sometimes people get educational degrees or become experts in specialized fields simply to enhance their egos. These individuals are less likely to share information or use their power for the sake of others.

Character power works in the same manner. Though people may assume that character power is always positive, it can in fact be negative. This type of power is given to an individual by a group, and the group looks at external behaviors to determine how "holy" or "ethical" an individual might be. Yet outward actions and attitudes don't always match the inner reality. On the surface, a person may exemplify a righteous life but be deeply flawed inside. The public persona and the private reality may be quite disparate. In the church, spiritual leaders may be tempted to use their character power for self-promotion. Character power can be used to enhance one's authority over others or to benefit others. If a person is self-aware and uses his or her character status to improve the lives of others, to care for others, to influence matters of justice, then character power is used in a positive way. Some individuals use character power to feed their own egos. If a person uses it to cover up a corrupt inner life or to manipulate others, character power is negative.

Role power can be used to reward, punish, or force someone to comply. Most people have experienced the punitive effects of a difficult boss or administrator who has power over jobs, vacations, benefits and advancement in the workplace. On the other hand, a boss who treats employees with kindness, fairness and personal attention makes it a joy to go to work. People who work or volunteer in Christian organizations likely have experienced both the negative and positive side of role power. Some find that leaders really do value their ideas and opinions. Others work tirelessly yet never receive recognition or encouragement from those in positions of influence.

Culture power can be a good thing when it is used to bring about positive change. For instance, because Americans highly value freedom, we sometimes get involved when we see that the rights of another group are being ignored or when we see suffering. Generally cultures are either open or closed. An open culture is willing to receive information from outsiders, to listen to contrary opinions and to examine its own motives and values. Open cultures make an effort to understand the concerns of other cultures. They respect their values and listen to dissenting voices. It is important to note that listening doesn't mean capitulation; rather, listening means understanding the implications of our actions. In the documentary film *The Fog of War,* former secretary of defense Robert McNamara outlines eleven lessons learned from the Vietnam War. The first one is to empathize with your enemy. Because he and others did not understand the source and depth of the North Vietnamese resolve to protect their country from "invaders," fifty-seven thousand Americans and two million Vietnamese—South and North, civilians and soldiers—died.[5] It was a tragic and costly misunderstanding of cultural values.

A closed culture refuses to listen to dissenting voices within it or receive new information from outside of it. Cultures that maintain a position of isolation and disregard internal and external problems use culture power negatively. Some Christian churches separate themselves from the rest of the world because they believe that things on the outside lead to evil. A closed culture takes on the role of an uninformed judge and is unable to empathize with those outside their group. In contrast, an open culture listens, learns and evaluates outside input.

Individuals or groups can have one or all of these powers. Figure 1 summarizes the four social powers and their potential positive and negative effects.

Social Power	Positive Effects	Negative Effects
Expert	Sharing knowledge; mentoring	Control; judgment
Character	Caring for others; justice	Manipulation; personal advancement
Role	Encouragement; networking	Punishment; exclusion
Culture	Open to growth and change	Closed to growth and change

Figure 1.

APPLYING THE SOCIAL POWER FRAMEWORK

Mark and Bess, Eileen, and Rick were in social power settings. What do their stories look like through this power lens? Obviously, Eileen did not have a sense of personal power. For some reason while growing up, her caretakers did not instill within her a sense of value and autonomy. Therefore, she was vulnerable to the abuse of power in relationships. Her social setting exacerbated the situation. Her husband, on the other hand, had lots of social power. He was an expert—a doctor. He had character power because he was respected as a successful doctor in the community and was a faithful church member. He had role power as a physician and an elder in his church. He had culture power because of his active involvement in the community and the money he gave to charity. But he had a hidden life. From Eileen's perspective, we see that he used his power to control, to enhance his ego, to punish Eileen and to avoid any substantive change. Because he had all the power, very few people really "saw" Eileen.

Mark and Bess are perhaps more typical. They were experts in their fields—Mark as a youth pastor, Bess as a secretary. They likely had character power because they were asked to serve on the search committee for a senior pastor. But their roles were not leadership roles, and their culture did not value their voice. They were too far down the totem pole. The committee missed a gold mine of wisdom by discounting the voices and concerns of those in less prestigious roles.

Rick had all four types of power and used them well. He had seminary training, giving him expert power. He had character power because his denomination ordained and supported him. His role was church planter, a tough leadership role. He came from a privileged family, which gave him culture power. Rick was aware of his privilege and power. He managed himself well. He instinctively understood that he had a good thing going, and he purposefully used that to serve others. He only needed to let go of his insecurities.

Jesus is our model for the redemptive use of power. He came as a servant and led as a Savior. He had all powers, both human and spiritual. Yet he allowed himself to be reviled, opposed and despised. He did not show bitterness or retaliate or retreat. He did not shrink from his mission to spread the good news of God's kingdom. How can we use our power as Jesus did? The Gospels tell many stories of encounters in which Jesus prevailed despite those who sought to bring him down. In the next chapter we will look at one of those stories and unpack how Jesus used his power, which gives us a model for the wise use of our own power.

QUESTIONS FOR DISCUSSION

1. Share a situation in which you had power, and describe how you felt. Then share a situation in which you had no power, and describe your feelings.

2. Which of the four social powers do you have? You may have different types of power in different areas of your life. How do you feel about the types of power you have? How do you exercise them?

3. Describe how you or someone else has exercised one of the social powers for negative or positive effect.

3

SIMON AND THE SINNER WOMAN

Jesus' Use of Power

Who is this who even forgives sins?

LUKE 7:49

Jesus had all four social powers. He was noted for his expertise with the Scriptures and for his ability to meet the challenges of his antagonists with logic, parables and probing questions. He was known for his righteousness, which gave him character power. At Jesus' trial, the secular governor Pilate, who was used to dealing with the political and criminal elements of his time, could find no reason to charge him. As a prophet, sage and healer, people flocked to Jesus to hear his teachings and be touched by his power. As a teacher, he had role power over his disciples, and as a prophet and sage, he had role power with the crowds. Wherever Jesus traveled, he used his power to catalyze a reformation of thinking about hospitality, outsiders, interpretation of the law, economic systems and the practices of the established religious system.

The Gospels often depict the Pharisees as foils to Jesus' righteous use of power. Like Jesus, these religious leaders had all four categories of power. But they used their power to maintain the current religious and social systems, reinforcing their interpretation of God's kingdom and their status and authority within the culture. They could not envision, much less welcome, the kingdom described by Jesus because too much was at stake—the loss of their power. They were fully invested in maintaining the existing system.

It can be difficult to tell whether someone is using social power for personal or social benefit. Conflict situations tend to bring out the true color of one's social power. Jesus often encountered conflicts about righteousness, as reflected in the keeping of the Jewish ceremonial laws. First-century Palestine was a culture of purity. Such a culture defines itself by what is sacred and strictly avoids what is profane. God called the Jewish people to be a kingdom of priests, to begin every prayer by remembering that the Lord God is one and that he is holy. Therefore, they were careful to differentiate between those things that were sacred and would align them with God's holiness, and those that were corrupt and would alienate them from God.

Holiness resulted in honor, and lack of holiness resulted in shame. Honor and shame were socially bestowed in public encounters, usually between men. The more honor one had, the more social power one had. The more shame one had, the more isolation and exclusion one would experience. Jesus continually challenged these traditional Jewish views on holiness because law keeping had become a symbol of status rather than devotion to God. The Gospels describe many conflict events between Jesus and religious leaders. During those events it was the crowd, not the participants, that decided who would gain or lose honor. By looking at these conflict events, we can see how Jesus used his social power in contrast to the way others used theirs.

THE STORY OF SIMON AND THE SINNER WOMAN

One of the Pharisees asked Jesus to eat with him, and he went into the Pharisee's house and took his place at the table. And a woman in the city, who was a sinner, having learned that he was eating in the Pharisee's house, brought an alabaster jar of ointment. She stood behind him at his feet, weeping, and began to bathe his feet with her tears and to dry them with her hair. Then she continued kissing his feet and anointing them with the ointment. Now when the Pharisee who had invited him saw it, he said to himself, "If this man were a prophet, he would have known who and what kind of woman this is who is touching him—that she is a sinner." Jesus spoke up and said to him, "Simon, I have something to say to you." "Teacher," he replied, "Speak." "A certain creditor had two debtors; one owed five hundred denarii, and the other fifty. When they could not pay, he canceled the debts for both of them. Now which of them will love him more?" Simon answered, "I suppose the one for whom he canceled the greater debt." And Jesus said to him, "You have judged rightly." Then turning toward the woman, he said to Simon, "Do you see this woman? I entered your house; you gave me no water for my feet, but she has bathed my feet with her tears and dried them with her hair. You gave me no kiss, but from the time I came in she has not stopped kissing my feet. You did not anoint my head with oil, but she has anointed my feet with ointment. Therefore, I tell you, her sins, which were many, have been forgiven; hence she has shown great love. But the one to whom little is forgiven, loves little." Then he said to her, "Your sins are forgiven." But those who were at the table with him began to say among themselves, "Who is this who even forgives sins?" And he said to the woman, "Your faith has saved you; go in peace." (Lk 7:36-50)

In Luke 7:36-50, Jesus is invited to the house of Simon the Pharisee for a meal, probably a gathering of the haburim, a fellowship group which provided moral support in the area of piety.[1] These events were open to the public, with the host and invited guests reclining around a central table, and the public seated or standing around the edges of the room.[2] A woman, described as "a sinner," also came to this gathering, intending to anoint Jesus after the traditional social graces were extended. Though very little is known about her besides her gender and social status, this unnamed woman had likely heard Jesus teaching and may have already experienced his acceptance, even if from a distance. She came to offer Jesus a gift of gratitude by anointing him, which was a risky and bold move on her part. It exemplified the measure of personal power she was beginning to feel. Jesus' words gave her hope that her life could be different.

Simon the Pharisee had every type of social power. As a Pharisee, he was considered a teacher and expert of the Torah, the Jewish law. Pharisees were often wealthy, giving them the leisure to adhere to every aspect of Jewish purity laws and codes. Simon's public adherence to the Jewish laws bestowed him with honor, and thus character power. As a man in first-century Jewish culture, Simon would have had role power over women, children and slaves in his household. The culture also valued and respected prophets, sages and teachers because of their ability to speak about God and to speak for God. Simon had every type of social power.

It is not clear whether Simon set up this event to unveil Jesus as an imposter or simply to interact with him out of curiosity. Whatever the purpose, Simon omitted the traditional hospitalities a host was to extend to his guests, such as a greeting with a kiss, washing of the feet and anointing with oil. The way these rituals were carried out told something about the power relationship between guest and host. For example, if the host kissed the guest on the cheek, it showed they were equals. If he kissed the guest's hand, it showed respect and honor. Kissing the feet would show that the host accepted the guest as his lord. In the same way, if the host provided the guest with water to wash his own feet, they would be considered equals. If the foot washing was done by a servant, the host showed respect for the guest. If the host himself washed the guest's feet, it showed service to the guest. The anointing with oil would be the final gesture and could symbolize the same corresponding relationships. Allowing the guest to anoint himself demonstrated equality. Having a servant anoint the head of the guest showed respect. The host stooping to anoint the guest's feet showed reverence. Perhaps because Simon is worried about the implications of these gestures in front of his peers, he omits them all. Simon did not welcome Jesus with any kind of kiss; he gave him no water for cleansing or oil for anointing. But Jesus was a gracious guest and did not take offense at being slighted. Instead, he ignored the omissions and reclined at the table without the welcoming rituals.

The sinner woman had come prepared to add her own perfume to the anointing at the end of the hospitality rituals. She observed the lack of hospitality and moved to make up for Simon's neglect. She used her tears to wet and wash Jesus' feet, her hair to dry them and her perfume to anoint him. The woman risked complete rejection by uncovering her hair because a woman's hair was considered to be erotic and was exposed only to her husband. For a sinner to touch the feet of a holy man was strictly taboo. The woman's position at Jesus' feet was a social gesture of complete service. No doubt some of the other guests snickered and some were offended, but most would have marveled at Jesus' response. Jesus dignified this sinner woman by allowing her to touch and serve him. Jesus' honor covered the shame of the woman. He showed his acceptance of her gesture of love and gratefulness.

Simon then had an opportunity to publicly challenge Jesus' honor. Simon thought to himself that Jesus was obviously not a prophet because he apparently could not discern that the woman was a sinner.

A true prophet would not contaminate himself by allowing a woman to touch him in public. Simon's inward attitude about Jesus might suggest his uncertainty on how to proceed with the meal because of the embarrassing event occurring in his house.

At this point Jesus did not address the woman, as one would expect, but turned to Simon. Jesus told a parable about two people who owed money to a creditor. One owed five hundred denarii, more than a year's worth of daily wages. The other owed fifty denarii, less than two months' wages. When neither of the men could pay, the creditor forgave their debts. Jesus then asked Simon, "Now which of them will love him more?" (Lk 7:42). Simon had no choice but to give the answer everyone in the room knew he had to: "I suppose the one for whom he canceled the greater debt" (v. 43). With this response, Simon exposed his own lack of hospitality. Simon had not given Jesus even the smallest gestures of welcome, which was an indication that he loved little. Jesus turned to the woman for the first time and detailed the quality of her hospitality compared to the lack of Simon's. Among first-century Jews, the quality of one's hospitality significantly reflected the quality of one's character.

Jesus' encounter with Simon and the sinner woman has to do with the economy of gratitude and forgiveness. The one who has sinned much and experienced much forgiveness also loves much. Jesus used the actions of the woman, the least in society, to shame the respected Pharisee Simon for his lack of action. Jesus' recognition of her public display of hospitality implied to the audience that she was the teacher of righteousness, and Simon was the sinner. In contrast to Jesus, Simon exercised his power to publicly judge Jesus and the sinner woman. He saw the woman as a reason for passing judgment, even if only in his thoughts. Simon was concerned with preserving his own status as a holy man and a Pharisee, at the expense of Jesus and the woman. Instead, he lost status, as everyone in the crowd recognized.

The audaciousness of the sinner woman's loving act illustrates the capacity of the powerless to influence change, if only someone in power publicly acknowledges the act. Jesus used his social power to restore the woman's identity. He acknowledged her and empowered her by elevating her status above Simon's. In front of the crowd, the holy man made the sinner woman holy. The woman with no power and no right to influence risked everything to thank Jesus for giving her hope. She gained the social power to change her status in the community. Jesus also used his power to expose Simon's lack of righteousness, not to condemn but to show compassion for the smallness of his world. Jesus gave Simon a chance to repent and confront his own self-righteousness.

The use of power by Jesus, Simon and the sinner woman is illustrated in figure 2. The "+" symbol means a positive use of power. The "-" minus symbol indicates a negative use of power. The "0" illustrates the absence of power.

	Expert	Character	Role	Culture
Jesus	+	+	+	+
Simon	-	-	-	-
Sinner woman	0	0	0	0

Figure 2.

Though Simon had all four types of social power, he used them in judgment to secure and preserve his own status and agenda. Jesus used his considerable social power in love to rebuke and teach Simon while restoring the woman. The woman who at the beginning of the story had no social power, who was the epitome of powerlessness, still chose to love much. Jesus accepted her act of love and announced her new status as a forgiven sinner. And she is remembered.

USING PERSONAL AND SOCIAL POWER FOR GREATER GOOD

Jesus was a person of no special appearance, but his impact was indelible. His power and authority astonished people. He used spiritual power to heal and social power to influence others toward a renewed understanding of God's kingdom. Jesus' use of power gives us a model for the righteous use of power. Jesus didn't use his power to zap Simon and punish him. He knew the seduction of using power for personal gain because he, too, was once tempted to misuse power.

In 1944, C. S. Lewis warned the students at King's College about the seduction of power. He referred to it as the "Inner Ring," where influence and success is offered to those who belong on the inside.

> You discover gradually that . . . it exists and you are outside it, and then later, perhaps you are inside it and the desire to be part of this Ring is one of the great permanent mainsprings of human action. . . . To nine out of ten of you the choice which will lead to scoundrelism will come, when it does come, in no very dramatic colours. . . . Over a drink or a cup of coffee, disguised as a triviality and sandwiched between two jokes . . . the hint will come . . . and you will be drawn in, if you are drawn in not by desire for gain or ease, but simply because . . . you cannot bear to be thrust back again into the cold outer world. . . . What the Inner Ring offers is what the serpent offered Eve: power . . . the knowledge that makes mere people into Gods.[3]

Simon belonged to the Inner Ring. He was important. He was righteous. But Jesus, by paying attention to small gestures and comments in public, exposed the true nature of Simon's power. I'm sure Simon thought his guest would be discussing theological ideas about the law, not using hospitality rituals as object lessons. Yet Jesus demonstrated that power used well works in small, simple ways, and power used well is redemptive.

Power is a neutral, natural and necessary component of influencing and leadership. Christians are designed to exercise power the way Jesus did. We are designed—as individuals and as a body—to influence others and ourselves toward a holy understanding of God's redemptive love. Our use of social power, whether we feel powerful or not, can trigger transformation toward holy wholeness. This use of power corresponds to Jesus' style of leadership.

Through the cooperation and empowerment of the Holy Spirit, the body can embrace the social aspects of power in order to grow the kingdom of God. In this way, each part of the body feels significant. Each contributes to the social power of the whole for positive impact. Therefore, we each have a responsibility to nurture and steward power, but leaders do especially. Leaders set the course and the tone. Simon misused his role as a leader. Perhaps some of the other guests around the table supported his actions, but Simon was the one on deck. It was his dinner party. He was the one Jesus engaged in conversation.

Power is God's gift. Powerlessness is not a virtue; rather, using power to help the powerless is. This is the true meaning of servant leadership. Jesus modeled this use of power over and over. If each member of his body is bold enough to use his or her power for good, then the negative use of power will become less frequent in the church and in the world.

QUESTIONS FOR DISCUSSION

1. What further observations do you have about the use of power by Jesus, Simon and the sinner woman?

2. Which of these three do you most relate to in your own understanding of power?

3. Look at another story of Jesus in public conflict, such as Matthew 12:9-14 or Luke 13:10-17, and discuss how the characters used their power.

4. How might the sinner woman's experience compare to the experience of Eileen from the previous chapter?

4

THE EPICENTER

How Leaders Take Up Space

We do not occupy space.
Space occupies us.
LEONARD SWEET

They said to him, "What did he do to you?
How did he open your eyes?"
JOHN 9:26

THE STORY OF JAMES AND BENNETT

James and Bennett attended a Bible college that was a Holiness school known for its distinctive theological perspective, which held that the second blessing—complete submission to the Holy Spirit in one's life—resulted in a person living a life free of sin and marked by love. The professors were warm, charismatic, bright and passionate about the ability of the second blessing to transform the church and American culture. Students could expect clear biblical teaching on the topic and testimonies of faculty members on Holiness living.

The school also prided itself on inviting students to participate in institutional discussions about goals and academic policies. James and Bennett were elected to serve as student representatives on the faculty committee. They were excited about the opportunity to experience the inner sanctum of the school's workings, and they had fresh ideas on improving chapel times and accountability groups. They looked forward to serving and being mentored by the faculty they had come to respect and admire.

Halfway through the first faculty meeting James and Bennett attended, a curriculum revision was introduced for discussion. The Biblical Studies Department proposed an increase in required Bible courses in order to strengthen the students' capacity to teach and preach accurately from the Bible. Previously collected feedback from graduates suggested this was an area for improvement. But to add more credit hours in biblical studies, the number of credit hours in theology would need to be cut back by six credits, or two courses. Suddenly the atmosphere changed from a calm, almost boring business meeting to an intense discussion between a few members of the faculty.

James and Bennett had decided beforehand to respectfully observe the first few faculty meetings until they understood how they were run and what was expected of them. They didn't expect to observe a heated discussion between an Old Testament professor and a systematic theology professor. Not only was it unexpected, it escalated. The theology professor became more and more animated and red in the face, accusing the Biblical Studies Department of undermining the other professors. The Old Testament professor responded with a personal jab, saying the other man was just insecure because he was the least effective faculty member. The others quickly intervened and tabled the discussion for a later date. But it was obvious to James and Bennett that the two professors had been at odds with each other for quite some time.

After the meeting, some faculty members attempted to minimize the conflict, saying the personalities of the two professors just didn't click. James and Bennett went to a nearby coffee shop and talked long and hard about what they had just observed. They were troubled by the disconnect between their experiences in the classroom and what they had just seen in the meeting room. What did it mean? Was holiness possible? How had these two professional, academic and spiritual men reached such a dead end in their relationship? And how were James and Bennett supposed to handle this? Should they just brush it off? They decided not to say anything about it to other students, but they became more discriminating about what they heard in the classroom.

SAM'S STORY

Sam had a successful house-painting company and served as an elder at a large church in Louisville, Kentucky. Because of his wealth, business savvy and commitment to the church, he was included on several important discussions about the future direction of the church. The pastor would often call Sam to ask his opinion about agenda items and staffing concerns. However, Sam's business employees were not so quick to seek his advice. Instead, they talked behind his back about his dishonest business practices and miserly way with the painters. Most of Sam's employees didn't go to church and thought Christianity was a farce. Sam would begin employee meetings with prayer, thanking God for blessing the company, but the painters saw him as a hypocrite. He often directed them to use cheaper paint or apply fewer coats in order to save the company money. Sometimes he would lie to a customer about being unable to finish a job because he was sending the crew over to another customer who was breathing down his neck.

When a leader's outside talk and inside walk are two different things, it has huge consequences for Christianity. This lack of congruence tells others that faith in Christ doesn't really change people. John O'Keefe, in a provocative online article, lists infighting, leadership bullies and lack of vision and change as reasons why church, in his words, "sucks."[1] Bono, of famed rock band U2, told an interviewer, "I'm not often so comfortable in church. It feels pious and so unlike the Christ that I read about in the Scriptures."[2] Mahatma Gandhi, the late Indian philosopher known for his activism through nonviolence, said about Christians, "I like your Christ; I do not like your Christians. Your Christians are so unlike your Christ."[3] Many people who have served in churches or worked in Christian organizations know that what is on the outside and what is on the inside can be very different.

James and Bennett looked differently at their school's faculty after the argument they witnessed. The professors probably would have been grieved by this unintended consequence. Sam, on the other hand, didn't seem to care that his employees had a different opinion of him than his pastor. He was still an important man at his church. These stories illustrate that the congruence of a leader's walk and talk is hard to ascertain unless you are on the inside. Only on the inside of a group or organization—only at the epicenter—can power and influence be observed in its raw form. The epicenter is where you can see whether power is being used for selfishness or servanthood.

YOU SAY YOU SEE

Despite having Christ in us, we are still finite human beings who make mistakes. We struggle with relationships, temptations and self-absorption. We struggle with how to use power and influence. We want to have integrity. We want to live and love as Christ did, but it's hard at times. Even the apostle Paul thought so. He wrote in Romans 7:15, "I do not understand my own actions. For I do not do what I want, but I do the very thing I hate." Sometimes our inability to be Christlike happens because, like Sam, we don't care.

But sometimes it happens because we are naive about our own hidden darkness.

In the 1960s psychologists Joseph Luft and Harry Ingham developed the Johari window, a model that illustrates the relationship between what we know and don't know about ourselves, and what others know and don't know about us. We all have a persona that we project and that others see in public, the "Arena." We also have things about ourselves that we hide from others, so we present a "Façade," or mask. Two other elements represent what is unknown to us. One is the "Blind Spot," what others see and know about us but we don't. This can be good, like when people see us as kinder than we see ourselves; or it can be bad, like when we are clueless about our problems. The final part is the "Unknown," both to others and to us. The Johari Window is depicted in figure 3.

	Known to me	*Not known to me*
Known to others	Arena	Blind Spot
Not known to others	Façade	Unknown

Figure 3.

The concepts behind the Johari window are not newly discovered by psychologists. Jesus in the first century understood our tendency to perceive ourselves in insular and self-protecting ways. The religious leaders of Jesus' day also had this problem. In the Gospel of John, Jesus spoke with a group of Pharisees who were questioning his healing of a man born blind: "Some of the Pharisees near him heard this and said to him, 'Surely we are not blind, are we?' Jesus said to them, 'If you were blind, you would not have sin. But now that you say, "We see," your sin remains'" (Jn 9:40-41).

The Pharisees believed they clearly understood God's kingdom and their role in it. They had dedicated their lives to it. However, Jesus was suggesting that because of the certainty of their belief that they *did* see, they were in fact sinners.

For Jesus, there is no sin in being blind. In other words, a lack of understanding, a lack of seeing, does not a sinner make. Jesus Christ is the light of the world, and we are his children of light. Just as people who are blind often must depend on others to provide guidance or assistance, we can only see with the help of Jesus. In Jesus' metaphor, those who claimed to see had forgotten to depend on God for their sight. The Pharisees constructed their understanding of the world so that they only needed God as a basis for devotion. They already saw. They already understood. They didn't need to listen to anyone else, not even to a great teacher and healer like Jesus—God himself, right in front of them. Their sin was focusing on the interpretation of God's kingdom rather than on God. They were locked in their own perspective. As long as their rules were followed, their world was orderly, and they were in power. Any leader can fall into the same trap. It's not hard to do, precisely because we are human and "we see through a glass, darkly" (1 Cor 13:12 KJV). So how do we avoid it? We begin by understanding how we are shaped by different types of social settings.

LEADERSHIP AND PHYSICAL SPACE

Our physical life is bound by physical space. Physical space is not abstract or neutral. It is a fundamentally dynamic reality. People are affected not only by the condition of their surroundings but also by the presence of others in that setting. In face-to-face interactions, the total body is involved. The physical, emotional, relational and cognitive parts are engaged.[4] The interaction is more than a mental process—it is a body process. Bodies bring meaning to a social setting.

We often think of a social gathering as the sum of the individuals present. If John, Hal, Cindy and George get together, we assume that John, Hal, Cindy and George are having a typical social gathering. But a gathering is more than the quantifiable and static presence of individuals in a given space at a given time. Space is alive and relational.[5] A person's identity in a particular gathering is directly influenced by the interactions that happen there.[6] For example, if John and Hal are best friends and they mainly talk to each other, Cindy and George might feel ostracized. If George is insecure and is ignored by the others, he might leave feeling even more convinced that he isn't worth much. If Cindy dislikes John, she might look for ways to undermine him instead of contributing positively to the group. In the spaces where we interact, we are constantly shaped and formed by what happens there.

Interactions in physical space define who is seen and heard and valued, and who is not; who has power, and who does not. Power is not brought into the space as an abstract concept. Each individual's sense of self is constructed in physical space. If Hal has an idea that everyone likes, he might go away thinking he has leadership potential. Power is constructed and communicated in physical space through interactions. Edward Soja, distinguished professor of geography and urban planning at UCLA, writes in his book *Thirdspace,* "We must be insistently aware of how space can be made to hide consequences from us, how relations of power and discipline are inscribed into the apparently innocent spatiality of social life, how human geographies become filled with politics and ideology."[7]

The importance of understanding the concept of spatiality is a particular characteristic of postmodern times.[8] Since space is relational, social life in physical space becomes a "complex web of relations of domination and subordination, of solidarity and cooperation. This aspect of space has been referred to elsewhere as a kind of 'power-geometry.'"[9] For instance, Jesus spent more of his time in small social spaces with his disciples than in the synagogue among the rabbis. Most of his teaching and work occurred outdoors. This showed that Jesus was accessible to all; he belonged to no one.

A prominent leader tells the story of visiting two different bank presidents within a few weeks' time. He and a friend showed up for their appointment with the first president. The secretary led them into a special room and brought them coffee, and then the president entered the room. At the meeting with the second bank president, the president himself invited them into his office and poured them coffee. The two bank presidents displayed two different power-geometries: one clarified the authority and role of the president, and the other invited the visitors into relationship.

Edward Hall, a researcher in the early 1960s, observed a correlation between personal intimacy and physical space, both in animals and humans. Hall and others found that individuals behave differently in different settings in order to protect or control. These actions could be recognized by the distance people maintained between each other in various settings. People automatically adjust the physical distance between themselves and others, usually without even being aware of it. These distances vary from culture to culture because of ethnic and social distinctives. Hall coined the term *proxemics,* meaning "hidden dimension," to describe the study of how humans use space. In 1968, Forston and Larson described proxemics as "the distance that man consciously or unconsciously maintains between himself and another person while relating physically to others with whom he is interacting."[10]

Westerners generally like to maintain personal space or a "bubble" around themselves, but it is adjustable depending on the circumstances. This bubble is observed in the distances we prefer to keep in our interactions with others. If physical distance isn't possible, then we may try to keep an emotional distance. For example, a person attending a movie might lay his jacket or her purse in the chair next to them. If that's not possible, such as when it's opening night and the movie is sold out, then people will generally hold themselves in, physically and emotionally, to avoid contact and interaction with others.

These distances indicate the level of intimacy people are comfortable having with others. When one person changes the distance, it can indicate something else. A person might move closer to intimidate or assert control and authority over the other person. A police officer or a drill sergeant might get in your face to make clear the line of authority. On the other hand, a change in distance could show a desire for intimacy, such as when one reaches out and takes the other's hand. The reverse indicates the opposite. Moving away instead of toward someone gives less of an appearance of control or a desire for intimacy.

Such body movements that change the distances between people are so instinctive that they are rarely thought about or talked about. Yet they have everything to do with power and influence. The statesman who told me I was only a workshop presenter moved into my personal space. He got close to me, using his body and voice to assert his authority. We can talk about power. We can make diagrams and offer definitions, even like I have in the previous chapters. But until we observe the actual interactions between individuals in social settings, it is just a lot of talk. In small social settings, the integrity of leadership is easily observed. The exercise of power gets more personal. Simon's public snubbing of Jesus was personal. Simon might have criticized Jesus all the time in front of his peers, but it became personal when Jesus was in his home.

The closer you are physically to another person, the more you engage the whole person. You can smell each other, look into each other's eyes, see the finer movements of the facial muscles, touch each other, talk more intensely. You can use your body to establish dominance or invite collaboration. The difference in physical space between people is important precisely because interpersonal communication cues are occurring. In order to unpack the relationship of space to influence, I will use the four basic types of space-keeping that Hall observed: public, social, personal and intimate.[11]

Public space. As people go about their personal pursuits in public space, they generally maintain a distance of at least twelve feet.[12] Though that distance cannot be maintained at all times, such as on a crowded sidewalk or in a lecture hall filled with students, it is the space people generally desire for public interactions. At that distance, there is little opportunity for accidental invasion of one's personal space or interruption of one's thoughts and purposes. People in a library do not want to be interrupted. Someone hurriedly running errands downtown usually does not engage with strangers. Public space can shift if people are experiencing something together, such as a rock concert or a worship service. In a shared group experience, talking with strangers is more likely to happen.

In most churches, worship is a public-space experience. Though worshipers might know each other, the act of worship is generally experienced individually. A certain level of anonymity is maintained. Speakers are not interrupted. Each individual is connecting to God (or not, as the case may be) through the music and words presented up front. Rarely, except in groups such as the Quakers, is worship intended for communal identity and connection. This does not mean that people don't experience increased feelings of belonging, but it is usually through one's own private thoughts and feelings. The people who lead the worship are the ones who talk and direct; the congregation follows. Therefore, even though public worship or other events that take place in a church, such as a vision night, are powerful ways to challenge and inspire, they rarely give individuals the opportunity to engage their inner self with that of another person. The emergent church movement sees this as a concern and addresses it with more casual worship settings and greater participation.

In public settings, the integrity of the individual in front—the pastor or leader—is difficult to accurately determine because it is based on audience observations rather than personal interactions. Even though a gifted speaker can inspire people to change their lives, the long-term cementing of that change depends on more intimate and consistent interactions. It is in more personal interactions that the use of power toward an individual or a small group is likely. And then it can be determined whether that power is being used for the benefit of others or for personal self-enhancement. This brings us from public space to social space, which is critical for seeing the body of Christ and the leaders of Christ in action.

Social space. Social space is observed in settings where people generally maintain a distance of four to twelve feet between each other. At this distance, you can see someone's face more clearly, you can speak in a normal tone of voice, but you are not close enough to touch. Social space occurs in settings where people have a common interest or purpose and where interaction is normal and expected, such as in meetings, parties, classrooms and fellowship times. People are focused on the same purpose, and they manage their participation in that space according to the group dynamics. For example, a person can use his or her body to guide the group's response by standing while the others are seated, or by leaning back in a chair and crossing his or her legs. Others will either feel that they are expected to listen or that they are invited to participate. Participants are still able to manage their own thoughts and feelings. They can better observe the finer body movements and facial expressions of other participants to discern whether it is a safe or unsafe environment.

Psychologically, people move from public space to social space when interaction occurs. An individual shares who she is or what he has to offer. People are less likely to use the protective masks they use in public space. People are more likely to talk and get to know each other in social space. The shorter distance encourages them to be authentic when sharing ideas and feelings. They are observed interactively rather than from an impersonal distance. For example, if you notice someone writing in a library book, you might wonder about his or her integrity. But if you spoke with that person, you would have the opportunity to find out whether he is careless, or she is destructive, or he is simply forgetful, or she bought the book from a library book sale. It becomes an informed understanding rather than an assumption. In social space, people have the ability to observe and to engage. Their true character can be seen. Those of sound character are given greater influence.

In the opening story, the faculty meeting James and Bennett attended was social space. The students observed the faces and actions of the professors and administrators around the table. They saw the disconnect between the walk and the talk of their leaders, and they were surprised. In the second story, Sam would boast on Sunday about his Christian business and then on Monday give his employees instructions to cheat a client. Social settings are the epicenter where the true nature of leadership is observed and evaluated.

Christian institutions are like any other institutions. There are meetings—lots of them. Committees or teams plan, make decisions, strategize and evaluate. They are small groups trying to get things done. If it is a high-functioning group, they might also experience feelings of closeness and greater energy by being together. They might pray and share things about their personal lives. They are able to move seamlessly from social space to personal space.[13]

Most people think meetings are boring and a waste of time, and they try to avoid them if possible. Leaders might get excited about an upcoming vision event or youth outreach or mission trip, but they often begrudge the energy and time spent in meetings to effectively plan the event. It seems as if meetings are the necessary evil, and God only comes out for the main event.

However, it's a myth that God moves primarily in public space rather than social space, such as meetings. It is in social space where God often moves in the hearts of those meeting together. It is in social space where the potential for deep change can occur because everyone's true character is observed and engaged. Individuals relax their guard and are more likely to move out of their private personal space. They invite others into relationship, or they establish dominance. It was only within the social space of the faculty meeting that James and Bennett could observe the broken relationship and resulting behaviors of the two professors. There was a disconnect between their public piety and their interpersonal interactions. When the members of a group have the same integrity on the inside that they display on the outside, then they are able to function as the very body of Christ.

In social space, it's harder for people to be uninvolved. Generally, the fewer the numbers, the greater the chance each person will take responsibility for the values and mission of the group. For example, if a church leader makes a plea for volunteers at the public worship service, it less likely to produce results than if the leader makes an appeal at each small-group gathering. Smaller groups have fewer absences and higher productivity, and they offer individuals the potential for higher satisfaction with their role.[14] Social space is where everyone in a group can see more clearly and be more engaged. Social space is also the boundary between public and personal space.

Personal space. Personal space is the preferred distance individuals maintain as their "bubble" of separation from others. This distance varies from culture to culture. Americans prefer a distance of two and a half to four feet, which can be seen as the distance between friends. At this close distance, visual contact is acute. Facial features, breathing levels, feelings of comfort or anxiety can all be intensely experienced by the other person.

When people move from social space into personal space, they usually want to be known better, to partner with others or to dominate others. In ministry settings, ideally the inner workings of a church or organization is a personal space in which individuals are invited to be known and to partner with others. Pastors, leaders and staff members feel free to use the closer space as an opportunity to grow, to be the body of Christ, to create safe relationships. Unfortunately sometimes even within Christian groups, moving from social space to personal space is done in an attempt to control or dominate individuals or groups.

Intimate space. Finally, intimate space is a distance of six to eighteen inches and is reserved for the closest of relationships, such as husband and wife, parent and child, and friends of the heart. At this distance in a safe and loving relationship, nothing is withheld. Your body and face can be completely relaxed. You can be yourself completely, without the need to withdraw, hide or protect. When the most intimate of relationships are used to dominate, it is the most destructive. Our bodies, and subsequently our psyches, cannot protect us. In the church and in Christian organizations, I believe that if the inner workings of social and personal space are holy and honest, full of integrity and grace, then it will profoundly influence what happens in the intimate space of families and other close relationships.[15]

POWER AND PHYSICAL SPACE

Because power is constructed through relationships in physical space, then naturally it is physically perceived through those interactions. We can observe power given or not given, received or not received, used well or used poorly. Because the interactions in physical space vary, the power dynamics also vary. The distances people keep between each other define the type of relational interactions they desire. Those relationships involve the exercise of power to either comfort or control.

As these spaces change, so does the exercise of power. Power exercised in personal or intimate space is not effective for influencing broad social change because these venues are individual and private. However, power exercised in social space is particularly dynamic, especially when there is the possibility of moving between personal and social space. The Gospels tell about Jesus in social and personal space. His teaching, preaching and healing happened in settings where people could see his face and experience the touch of his hand. Hospitality events, such as meals, were key occasions to see the power dynamics between Jesus and the others who were present. Because social space is the boundary between public and personal space, people are relationally oriented, either as participants or as observers and interpreters. Individuals are no longer anonymous, and a pecking order is established.

A deep connection exists between physical space and the way we see ourselves and others. The closer people get physically, the more potential there is for them to have a positive or negative impact on each other. Public space allows you to see and hear a leader but rarely to truly know him or her. For James and Bennett and for Sam's employees, the inner social space experiences were revealing. In social space, such as meetings, we truly see ourselves and others. The way power is used in these smaller settings is the true measure of a leader's integrity. In the long run, how the group gets along in the meeting room is more important than how they get along in public. How leaders use power in close quarters is a more significant indication of integrity than what they do or say from a pulpit or speaker's platform.

QUESTIONS FOR DISCUSSION

1. Share an experience when you observed a disconnect between a leader's public persona (public space) and his or her behavior

in a meeting (social space). Then share an experience when you observed the opposite—complete congruity. How did the two experiences affect you?

2. How do you act differently in your public spaces, social spaces, and private spaces?

3. In meetings at your ministry or workplace, are you able to enter into personal space, or do you stay in social space (or even public space)?

4. Why do you think power is observed more easily in social space? How have you observed the impact distance has on people in the different types of space?

5. How have you observed other cultures' use of different types of space?

5

THE "IT" FACTOR

Power in Presence

She's one of only a couple of people in
the competition who has the "it" factor.
She's not too nerdy-looking.
COMMENT POSTED ON IDOLBLOG

On the sabbath he began to teach in the
synagogue, and many who heard him were
astounded. They said, "Where did this man
get all this? What is this wisdom that has
been given to him? What deeds of power
are being done by his hands!"
MARK 6:2

Princess Diana was one of those women who had presence, who
drew everyone's attention whenever she walked into a room. A man
who had been at a party where Princess Diana was in attendance
said, "There was something about her that was effervescent. You

couldn't help but stare. She was the most beautiful woman I've ever seen." This capacity to draw the attention of others is often referred to as "presence" or the "it" factor. Some equate presence with *gravitas*, which comes from a Latin word meaning "heavy." Gravitas can be described as an appearance of dignity, influence or authority, and it is a type of presence often seen in politicians and academics.[1] The "it" factor is attributed to people who seem to have something special about them, something that sets them apart. It isn't easy to define. Individuals as different from each other as the Dalai Lama, a nonmaterialistic spiritual leader, and Paris Hilton, a materialistic party girl, have been described by different people as having the "it" factor. If someone consciously uses this quality to get attention or to influence others, it becomes charisma. Bill Clinton, for example, is known for his charisma. He is tall, intelligent and outgoing, and when he walks into a room, everyone knows he's got "it," no matter what their political views or moral opinions about his character.

Princess Diana was a beautiful and captivating woman. She couldn't go anywhere without being noticed, without being watched. Living under that type of pressure is difficult. Public figures seem to both love and hate the constant scrutiny of the public. Often the scrutiny is more than curiosity or a pastime, and it results in mimicry. People copy the celebrity's fashion, hairstyle and mannerisms, and if the celebrity is so inclined, he or she can influence people to support certain causes and political agendas.

On the other end of the spectrum are individuals who are rarely noticed. In the Broadway hit *Chicago,* Roxie Hart's husband, Amos, has zero "it" factor. He bemoans the fact that no matter what he does or says, he is not taken seriously or noticed by others. He feels invisible and inconsequential. In the number "Mr. Cellophane," he sings:

If someone stood up in a crowd
And raised his voice up way out loud

And waved his arm and shook his leg
You'd notice him

If someone in the movie show
Yelled "Fire in the second row,
This whole place is a powder keg!"
You'd notice him

And even without clucking like a hen
Everyone gets noticed, now and then,
Unless, of course, that personage should be
Invisible, inconsequential me!

Cellophane
Mister Cellophane
Shoulda been my name
Mister Cellophane
'Cause you can look right through me
Walk right by me
And never know I'm there. . . .[2]

In the research world, there are various kinds of presence, some having to do with mental presence, others with social presence. The kind of presence we will discuss here is not so much about a person's awareness of his or her context but about the impact that person brings into an environment. This chapter is about the power that comes with presence, and the lack of power that comes with its absence. Though presence or the "it" factor is easy to observe in larger-than-life personalities, here we will focus on the subtler forms of presence. We will examine the impact of a leader's presence on his or her ability to influence others in social settings.

THE STORY OF JASON AND FRANK

At a meeting of the entire sixteen-member staff of Grace Community Church, the pastor introduced a controversial strategic plan to get the church involved in community service. The plan called for developing a halfway house for male inmates released from the state prison about thirty miles south of town. A church taskforce had investigated several possible service opportunities and determined that the halfway house would meet real needs, both for these men and for the state. There were only a few such places within a hundred-mile radius of the prison, and the ones that existed were filled to capacity. Most of the inmates had been convicted of drug trafficking, sex crimes or robberies.

The discussion that followed the taskforce's presentation was intense. Some vocal individuals praised the incarnational opportunity this proposal would have for Grace Community. Others, just as vocal, believed it would be too much of a stretch and would put the church community at risk to serve sex offenders and drug dealers. After a couple hours of back-and-forth, it became clear the staff needed more time to process the issue. Over the next few days, staff members rehashed the topic at lunch, in the halls and in one another's offices. Jason, the adult ministries pastor, was inundated with coworkers wanting to share their perspectives. But Frank, one of the small-group fellowship pastors, felt overlooked. During lunch one day, Sharon, another small-group pastor, said to Frank, "Frank, you should have been at the meeting. It was tense."

"I was there," Frank said.

"Oh, I'm sorry. I didn't see you."

If this were but one occasion of being overlooked, Frank probably wouldn't have thought too much about it. But for Frank, variations on this scenario happened over and over again. After worship, social events and meetings, others would tell him what happened as if he hadn't been there. Frank knew that this cloak of invisibility hurt him as leader of his small-group ministry. Group members didn't return his e-mails. They didn't respond well to his suggestions or seek him out for spiritual counsel as often as he would have liked. In fact, people sometimes asked to be moved to another fellowship group. Frank found this humiliating and disturbing. He knew that his ministry position was tenuous, and he didn't understand what was going on. He loved God with everything in him. He was pious and kind. He had put himself and his family into debt getting the best seminary preparation. God had called him into ministry. Why did he feel so unused and undervalued at Grace Community?

Jason, on the other hand, was sought out for all sorts of conversations. People would often wait until Jason arrived before beginning a meeting, or they would reschedule it to make sure he could attend. People relaxed when he walked in the room. His calendar was full of appointments. And he wasn't even the senior pastor. This was getting to be a problem, and Jason knew it. He had more influence than he knew what to do with. People wanted to know what he thought, and when he spoke, they listened. His calendar was so full, it was sometimes hard to find time to think. He knew he was on the edge of a dangerous place because he realized that he liked it. He liked mattering to others so much that they sought him out first. He liked giving the impression of being important. He wrestled with feelings of pride in his prayers.

When Frank spoke, people would listen halfway and move on. He had good things to say, but it didn't seem to matter. In meetings, Frank had offered ideas that others missed until Jason repeated them later. Then the group would notice and attribute the idea to Jason. No one, not even Jason, appeared to remember that Frank had said it first.

How could Frank lead like Jesus if no one paid attention to him? How could Jason lead like Jesus if people paid too much attention to him? Christians bear the light of Christ, but how will others see Jesus if no one notices you? How will they see him if your light is so dazzling it overshadows the image of Christ?

PHYSICAL ELEMENTS OF PRESENCE

Presence is the visual manifestation of power carried in the body that has an influencing effect on others in social settings. Presence is deeply connected to power. The more presence you have, the more influencing capacity you have. People with presence have the ability to walk into a room and get the attention and respect of its occupants. Jason had it; Frank did not. Jesus had it too. Crowds followed him. Synagogue leaders and rabbis wanted to talk with him. A Roman centurion sought him out for help. Jesus' words and actions were astonishing and memorable, and he challenged the views of the prevailing religious culture on such topics as holiness and hospitality.

Presence is intuitively perceived by a group. A person brings it with him or her into a group, and it is acknowledged by the group. Both elements are necessary. A person expects it or seeks it or cultivates it, and the group responds to it. People notice presence. The manner in which a person carries and positions his or her body, the subtlety of facial expressions and the distance kept from others reflect attitudes as clearly as words spoken. Marshall McLuhan said, "The medium is the message," but in leadership the body is the message.[3]

The closer the quarters in physical space, the easier it is to take in and process all the physical cues. The finer movements of the face and body can be observed. Evaluating presence can tell you a lot—not everything, but a lot—about someone else and their place in a group. Every social group unconsciously trains its members to ascertain instinctively who belongs and who doesn't, who is strong and who isn't. A Sunday school teacher once asked her class of eleven seventh- and eighth-grade girls whether there was a pecking order in the group. One girl went to the board and wrote it out from number one to eleven. Everyone, including the teacher, knew that it was an accurate reflection of how the girls interacted with each other.

Presence is a package of both fixed and fluid physical elements. Some markers of presence cannot be altered: gender, age, body type, facial features, race. Consider the impact of an average-looking, middle-aged female walking into a roomful of male leaders. Her presence will be taken in and processed in microseconds. The presence of a good-looking young man walking into a predominantly female college Bible study group will be taken in and processed in a different way. Not only do people notice and evaluate an individual's presence, they also experience an emotional reaction based in part on these fixed physical elements.

The fluid physical elements of the presence package are just as powerful. These might include economic status, personality, level of education, social skills, spirituality, sense of purpose and self-confidence. These are also carried and expressed in the body. Taken together, these fixed and fluid features impact others viscerally and create presence. Someone who is strikingly attractive but displays surly and withdrawn body language might be noticed but probably won't gain the power to influence. On the other hand, a nondescript individual who moves confidently into a room and greets others with a firm handshake will instantly create presence.

Though created in the image of God, we live in a very physical world in very physical bodies. Your body carries and expresses your capacity for influence. It projects your presence in concrete, measurable ways. People use all their physical senses to evaluate you. They scan and observe your face, not just for details like eye color but for cues as to whether you are safe or unsafe, whether you belong to the group or not. They hear what you say, both in the tone of your voice and in the words you choose. All of these elements add up to concrete, measurable information about who you are and whether or not you will influence the group.

Presence is complicated by the other side of the equation—that it is interpreted by others. You might feel that you have plenty of presence, but unless others perceive it and recognize it as a group, it has little value for influencing. To create presence, there must be a marriage between your physical elements and the reception of the group. The communication signals exchanged must be on the same bandwidth.

Like power, presence is neutral, and it is a gift. Like power, presence can be used for healthy or unhealthy reasons. If you use your presence to increase your status and influence for personal gain at the expense of others, then it is unhealthy. If you use your presence to influence like Jesus did, then it is healthy.

While vacationing on Maui a few years ago, my husband, Randy, and I encountered two very different, very memorable people. The first we met at a stunning scenic overlook off Route 30 above Honolua Bay. We had pulled off the highway and were watching the boaters and snorkelers in the bay below when another car pulled into the overlook area. A young couple got out and joined us at the edge. The woman turned to us and said brightly, "Hello, nice people! Where are you from?"

I answered, "Portland, Oregon. And you?"

"Charlotte, North Carolina."

She had a camera in her hand, so I asked, "Would you like us to take your picture?"

"Yes, we would. Portland must be where all the smart people are. Thank you!"

What struck me about this woman was her openness and warmth. She had a contagious, safe energy about her presence. We felt even happier after a short conversation as we discovered they were on their honeymoon and we shared that we were on our anniversary trip. Afterward, Randy and I talked about how she was the kind of person you would look forward to seeing because she brought such life with her.

Later that evening we attended the Warren and Annabelle magic show in Lahaina. At each show, four "lucky" couples get to sit up

front and be part of the show. Warren begins the show by talking
with those couples as the audience witnesses the banter. He began
with the couple to his right.

"What do you do for a living?" Warren asked the husband.

"I'm a designer of stealth jets."

"No, you're not, because you couldn't tell me if you were."

"I have an investment business."

"Is it doing good?"

"Oh, yeah, really good."

Warren turned to the wife and asked, "What's your name?"

"Adiel."

"Huh?"

"Like Ariel, but with a *d*. It's my stage name."

"Are you an actress?"

"Kinda."

"Kinda?"

"I do stand-up improv."

"Have you been onstage?"

"Oh yeah, lots of times."

"Where?"

"Comedy Central."

"How many times?"

"Lots."

"Okay. Give me a joke."

"It's improv. I'm taking classes."

"Oh, so you've been onstage a lot in your classes. What's your real
name?"

"Tifny."

"Tiffany?"

"No, *Tifny*. Pronounced with two syllables, but spelled the same."

This couple was also memorable, but in a different way from the
newlyweds. Either "Tifny" and her husband had decided to play-act

for Warren, or they were trying to exude more status than they actually had. Perhaps they intended to inflate their presence to have fun, or they wanted to project their self-importance in front of others. Either way, Tifny and the woman from Charlotte provide excellent illustrations of how brief encounters can create presence that is experienced by others either as engaging or as disingenuous.

PRESENCE AND CHARISMA

Presence comes in varying intensities. Charisma is presence at full throttle. *Charisma* comes from the Greek word *charis,* which means "divine gift." Charismatic leaders use emotional appeal to influence their followers. The emotional connection can become so strong that charismatic leaders may even be able to motivate people to harm themselves, such as Jim Jones did when he led his followers to commit mass suicide in 1978. Other charismatic leaders use their vibrant presence to catalyze positive transformation, such as Martin Luther King Jr. did in the Civil Rights movement.[4]

Charisma, like power and presence, is a neutral quality. We love it, yet we are suspicious of it. We like leaders who are confident and passionate, but we are wary of leaders who are highly emotional and use the influence of their personality to persuade.

Charismatic leaders influence through emotional appeals based in self-confidence that stems from an unshakable conviction in the rightness, even righteousness, of their beliefs. These same convictions are held by the followers, whose commitment to the leader validates his or her values and goals. These leaders are often perceived as heroes. Bono of U2 fits this description. The force of his convictions and goals to eradicate poverty and disease, coupled with his international appeal as a great musician, have given him a platform for effecting tremendous social good. Charismatic leaders create meaning for others. They say what others feel, and they say it very well.

Some say that Jesus had charisma, and that special gift helped make him a great influencer. Jesus certainly captured the imagination of many people. He definitely had immense powers and unshakable conviction in his vision of God's kingdom. And the crowd followed him, even to the foot of the cross. Though some could not stomach his ideas, many others did. This image of Christ's charismatic leadership is inspiring as well as daunting. How can we possibly follow in his footsteps? If we try, aren't we setting ourselves up for disappointment and failure? It's easy to believe that there are only a few special people to whom God gives presence and charisma and the ability for great leadership—and maybe the rest of us should only expect a modest capacity to influence.

However, charisma is only one type of presence—kind of like presence on steroids. Yes, some have it and some don't. But charisma is not necessarily a predictor—nor a requirement—of good leadership. Having it does not mean that a person will use his or her power wisely. Lacking it does not prevent a person from cultivating presence in order to influence like Jesus.

PRESENCE AND POWER

We are made in the image of God. God's own presence is within us wherever we go, whatever we do. Presence, like power, is a natural God-given birthright. Each person brings his or her presence into a social setting. Each member of the body is part of the sacred, incarnational presence of Christ. Each of us has the responsibility to bring our Christlikeness to the group. Each of us has the responsibility to manage the visibility of our presence. Jesus did not say that some of us are little lights, some are spotlights and some are flickering lights. He said we are each the light of the world, particularly when we are in community.

A woman who had been on the top leadership team of a large international organization for twenty years shared with me that in all those years during the monthly meetings, she didn't say anything. How is it possible that, for such a long time, no one needed her words, her insights, her expression of herself as part of the team? To make matters worse, it appeared that no one noticed. She was the Mr. Cellophane in that group. Not that she didn't contribute good work or that people didn't like and appreciate her—quite the contrary. Mr. Cellophane is often loyal, hard-working, nice. But wouldn't this woman's perspective have added something important to the organization? When I asked her why she kept silent all those years, she answered, "It was so hard to get to the top. I didn't want to rock the boat and lose it all." So she was there, but not there. Without having presence in a group, there is little or no influence.

Presence is the visual and visceral effect our bodies have on others. Those with a strong presence are instinctively given more power to influence. Ultimately it doesn't matter what we look like. It matters how we handle ourselves in a group.

The following story takes place within a denomination going through extensive change. The superintendent of the denomination, who is leading the change, has neither charisma or the "it" factor, but he does have presence. Under this superintendent's guidance, the denomination is in the process of updating its entire structure to twenty-first-century ways of handling its business and ministries. To change the structure of an entire denomination that holds little control at the local level is nearly an impossible undertaking, especially when the group's polity requires group decision-making processes. The success of such a huge transition can be undermined by special-interest groups, the group in power or members of the group who use influence in unhealthy ways. In this case, everyone agreed that they needed to change. So in order to change, everyone agreed to give everything up. Every committee was dissolved. Every budget was given up. All existing committee chairs and members resigned. All the local leadership positions were closed, and those people lost their jobs. Do you realize how amazing that is? Imagine your own church, denomination or ministry organization doing the same thing.

As I talked with a respected pastor in this denomination, I marveled at how well the process was going. I asked him why he thought it was going so well, and he said, "I'm sure the Holy Spirit has a lot to do with it, but if I had one word to say about it, I would say *size*. The superintendent's small physical size and his laid-back, unruffled, open personality are the reasons why it's going well. He's so nonthreatening." The superintendent is five feet three inches tall. He wears Birkenstocks and casual clothes. He listens intently to others. He loves the people, the denomination as a whole, and its leaders and pastors. He is centered in Christ, which brings a peaceableness to his presence. He is a nonthreatening servant leader, so people trust the process of change that he is leading.

Most of us don't think much about the signals our bodies give in groups. As a result, we sometimes underestimate or overestimate our impact. If everyone has presence, how do we decipher it and manage it in order to use our influence to benefit the group, like the denomination superintendent did? The next chapters address this question.

QUESTIONS FOR DISCUSSION

1. When you walk into a social setting, do you feel more like a person with the "it" factor or more like Mr. Cellophane? In a meeting, on which end of the continuum do you find yourself?

2. Explore what happens emotionally and spiritually to people with a "cellophane" presence. Explore what happens emotionally and spiritually to people with the "it" factor.

3. Have you known any charismatic leaders? What was your experience with them? Do you think Jesus was a charismatic leader? If so, what characterized him as such?

4. How important do you think presence is for being the light of Christ to others?

6

THE LAW OF THE JUNGLE

Visual Marks of Presence

[The authors] show a lion in his winter.
LISA MILLER, SPEAKING OF BILLY GRAHAM,
IN A REVIEW OF *THE PREACHER*
AND THE PRESIDENTS

**[Jesus] is the image of the invisible God,
the firstborn of all creation.**
COLOSSIANS 1:15

We have an innate survival instinct that helps us distinguish between the mighty and the meek. The mighty can be dangerous; the
meek, not so much. In the jungle, the lion is unequaled. He is the
king, and he is feared. He looks ferocious with his mighty mane and
sounds ferocious with his roar. Our bodies, too, can communicate
either mightiness or meekness. Leaders know this instinctively. Sir
Richard Branson, a global adventurer and entrepreneur, created a reality TV show called *Rebel Billionaire*. Its purpose was to take a group

of young business entrepreneurs on a world adventure to test their business acumen and strength of character. Ultimately Sir Richard offered a million-dollar prize to whichever contestant demonstrated the same spirit as Sir Richard had on his way to becoming a billionaire. Although the contestants didn't know specifics about the prize, they did know something big was at stake. In the opening show, Sir Richard disguised himself as an unkempt taxi driver to pick up the contestants at the airport. He portrayed himself as an elderly, disheveled man to see how the contestants would treat him. Most completely ignored him. Three treated him poorly, making fun of his appearance or being rude when he talked to them. Imagine their surprise and embarrassment when Sir Richard revealed himself.

If we are honest, no one is exempt from some measure of discrimination. We all tend to dismiss some people and pay attention to others. Sir Richard was still Sir Richard, but dressed as an old taxi driver, with rumpled clothes, stooped posture and shuffling walk, the contestants assumed he was not important. Though they all knew what Sir Richard looked like, they didn't recognize him in disguise. Throughout the rest of the show, Sir Richard usually dressed casually, and everyone gave him their full attention and complete respect.

First impressions are powerful. Our presence matters when we walk into a room. People make decisions based on physical presentation. This is problematic for Christians who are taught through the example of Christ to pay attention to the marginalized, the poor and the alien. It is also a problem for those who believe Christians are called to a simpler lifestyle to avoid the trappings of a consumeristic culture like the United States. Christians know better than most that what is on the inside matters eternally, and what is on the outside will fade and die.

How do we use presence, and the power that comes with it, in ways that enhance the kingdom of God? How do we tell the good news through the use of our bodies so that others are influenced toward Christ?

This chapter does not give tips for how to "dress for success" or use "body moves for power"; just the opposite. Creating presence isn't about glitzy manipulation for personal benefit. It's about attentive awareness for the benefit of others. Deciphering presence gives us another resource for taking responsibility for the power that comes with it. The human body is part of the leadership process. It cannot be ignored, especially in group settings. We need a format for talking about it honestly together. The purpose of this chapter and the next is to present clearly what most of us instinctively understand about the impact our presence makes in a group. Then we can talk about it, and then we can learn to steward it.

Presence is a complicated package of the tangibles and intangibles we carry in our bodies: the visuals, or what we see; and the viscerals, or what our bodies experience. Mother Teresa was a very small woman, barely five feet tall. She always wore the same clothing as a nun in the Missionaries of Charity order, a white habit with blue trim. From 1948 until her death in 1997, she served the most neglected, the poorest of the poor in India. Yet she became so well-known for her work that she received the Nobel Peace Prize in 1979. Though petite in size, common in appearance and serving as a nun at the bottom of the power "food chain," she inspired thousands to commit to something grander by serving the desperately poor and dying. Though she did not dress for success or orchestrate her movements in order to have power and influence, she had both nonetheless. The visceral impression she made grabbed everyone's attention. In the same way, Jesus was an ordinary man with little social status as a carpenter, yet his presence greatly influenced others. Something more than first impressions and outside appearances matters.

The amount of presence you have is not determined from birth. Otherwise Mother Teresa would have had little impact. Presence isn't a manufactured effect or a commodity of the privileged, although some act as though it were. Some people self-identify as wallflowers or introverts. They expect to spend their lives as a spot on the wall, and they are content to do so. Others are high-flyers and expect the opposite. They seek to be the center of attention, and they suffer when they are not. However, the experience of presence isn't simply a matter of attitude. It is interactive.

Since presence is the visceral-influencing effect a person has on others in social interactions, the visuals are what others notice first. These are the basic characteristics of gender, age, appearance, race, etc. (see figure 4). These visual markers provide the first impression of who a person is. A group unconsciously begins to create a pecking order as soon as someone walks in and says hello.

Before we get into the specific visual markers, there are four things to remember about them. First, visuals are culturally influenced. For instance, in Asian cultures older people are highly respected, while in Western cultures the elderly are sometimes patronized or dismissed. In many of today's mainline denominations and in corporate settings, gender is less of an issue than in church settings where only males can serve in leadership positions. Second, the value placed on these visual markers can vary from one group to another. Education usually gives someone expert power. However, some groups might dismiss an expert because they are suspicious of his or her knowledge. Third, an individual within a group may have different values than the group as a whole. For example, one person is uncomfortable with someone who is dressed fashionably while the rest of the group is impressed. However, every group seems to have an overriding collective consciousness about who is qualified to have influence. Fourth, over time the amount of an individual's presence in a group can change, becoming greater or lesser.

The visual markers listed in figure 4 represent general Western values. When added up, they usually indicate who has more presence—and thus who takes up more space—in a social setting. They provide guidelines for discerning who most likely does and does not have power to influence. They are not meant to determine whether someone should be given power or not.

More Presence	Less Presence
Male	Female
Dominant culture	Nondominant culture
Extroversion	Introversion
Middle age (for men); youth (for women)	Old age
Good looks; attractiveness	Ordinary physical features
Wealth; fame	Poor or middle class; unknown
Well-dressed	Unexceptionally dressed
Higher education	Little education
Married	Single
Role authority; corner office	Under authority; cubicle

Figure 4.

GENDER

Connie graduated from seminary at the top of her class. She won the preaching award. She demonstrated leadership gifts. Though on paper her denomination supported women in ministry, they were reluctant to give her a senior pastor position. Connie received a post to a small, dying rural church that had about fifteen to twenty regular attendees. One of her fellow pastors commented that at least she couldn't mess it up. A male colleague of Connie's, who graduated at the same time but who had struggled academically and socially, was given a thriving church of three hundred members. Within two years, Connie's church had grown to one hundred members. Her colleague's church was floundering, and attendance was dropping. He left his church and ministry after two years. Here the primary determiner of which church the graduates would be placed in was gender rather than leadership ability or preaching skills.

Gender is the most obvious and primary of distinctions made in social groups. Gender is linked to perceptions about a person's role and status in the group. Gender is also linked to each culture's assumptions about what it means to be female and what it means to be male. Susan Hanson and Geraldine Pratt, research professors of geography, concluded, "The experience of being a man or a woman is different, depending on where one lives, because different types of jobs, with different scheduling opportunities, are locally available. . . . It is important to note this geographical variation because it underlines the point that gender divisions and experiences are socially constructed."[1]

The mistake of assuming that a female is in a lower position of authority than a male happens precisely because these assumptions about role and status are deeply ingrained by the culture. Males are usually given more influence than females for two reasons: males tend to take more up more physical space, and the culture gives them more space. In a study at the University of Arizona, researchers found that men were less likely to share workspace than women, and women had trouble getting research space for a lab.[2] Another study demonstrated that even with all the Title IX opportunities given to girls in physical education and sports, boys still got better sports equipment and the optimal locations and times for their games and practices.[3] One educator said that when the boys' and girls' baseball teams of his Midwest school traveled to away games on the same bus, the girls were dropped off at a fast-food restaurant for dinner while the boys were taken to a sit-down restaurant.

Women in leadership are often disadvantaged simply because of their gender. Even though women have the same leadership capacities and the same willingness to work as hard as men, they are often given less authority and fewer decision-making roles.[4] Even when females are perceived as having the same amount of dominance as males, the males still get higher rewards. On performance ratings, domineering males get higher scores, regardless of whether males or females are evaluating them. If men use threatening or obtrusive behavior, such as speaking loudly or pointing fingers, they get away with it because their behavior is interpreted as commanding and leaderlike. Domineering males get more respect than strong females. Strong females often receive harsher criticism on performance evaluations.[5] It is a well-documented fact that males are valued more than females even in the United States, and males are given more power to influence.[6] In their review of the research, Cecilia Ridgeway and Chris Bourg, social science faculty members at Stanford, summarized the situation this way: "The effects of gender status beliefs on any given encounter are often modest and so taken for granted as to be unrecognized by the participants. Yet these effects accumulate as they are repeated over multiple contexts and encounters to create significant inequalities in men's and women's social outcomes in society."[7]

The result is that males and females often feel as if they live in two different worlds—one for men and one for women.[8] When a woman is in a setting primarily occupied by men (or vice versa), it is a cross-cultural experience. If one culture, such as the male culture, is dominant and the other is not, it creates an imbalance. The member of the nondominant culture is always at a disadvantage and so might try to adapt to the dominant culture's modus operandi.

Early in the feminist movement, women trying to break through the glass ceiling would sometimes adopt the same type of dress and aggressive-competitive behaviors as men. So some women in top leadership positions were competitive and petty, and even then would still pay more attention to male voices than to female voices.[9] Women wonder if they need to adopt the dominant culture's ways in order to be heard—they don't. But they will likely experience difficulties until they establish trust within the group. Reacting to the dominant culture or adopting its ways is counterproductive in the long run.

An Air Force colonel related to me that she began her career with several other young female officers. Almost all of them experienced some form of discrimination or sexual harassment. Most of the women tried to cope by becoming buddies with the male officers and adopting more masculine body stances. The colonel purposefully chose to retain her femininity, which irked her female companions, by wearing lipstick, nail polish and earrings. She wanted to be who she was—a woman serving as an officer in the Air Force. She did experience discrimination, and she was passed up for promotion several times because she reported male officers who sexually harassed her. In the end, however, she surpassed the rank of her fellow female officers as well as many of the males. Her success came because of her ability to bring who she was, not who others thought she should be, to the setting.

CULTURE

Culture is the shared patterns of behaviors, ideas, values and symbols held by a group. These patterns distinguish one group from another. For example, flags represent a country's values. But even within a country various ethnicities can differentiate subcultures. Usually one culture is dominant, while others are not.

If a person is female and a member of a nondominant culture, she has two hurdles to overcome: gender and race. A female African American doctor wrote about her experiences in a *Newsweek* article called "My Black Skin Makes My White Coat Vanish."[10] She tells how several times people assumed she wasn't a doctor, despite the white coat stitched with her name, Dr. Lumumba-Kasongo. Once while dining at an upscale restaurant, her friend started choking. Other diners kept yelling for a doctor, despite her assurances that she was one, and they didn't stop until two white males came rushing over.

By this time, Dr. Lumumba-Kasongo had successfully dislodged the food from her friend's throat. The two white men assured the crowd that the choking victim was okay and that the African American woman was indeed a doctor.

Years after the Civil Rights movement, we still carry ingrained cultural perceptions about members of other races and cultures. These perceptions are so embedded in our minds and bodies that we are often unaware of them. Some build up over a lifetime. Some become ingrained after a single catastrophic event, such as 9/11. I've always had the habit of wrapping my head in a black scarf to keep warm in the winter, and I often combine it with a long black coat and black shoes. No one paid any attention to me until after 9/11, and then I started getting angry stares.

When we cross the boundaries of race or culture, either to visit or to work, we often experience culture shock. This involves an inability to correctly interpret the various nonverbal cues people use to interact with others in social settings. When our body is not comfortable in crosscultural situations, we are constantly trying to understand all the social cues. This is even more difficult when there are other variables in play, such as gender or economic factors: "Cultural variations are hard to unravel because . . . these variables are not isolated behaviors but patterns of interactions with interpretations of their meaning. Persons are able to reveal more details about the patterns of groups they interact with frequently and gloss over details with groups they interact with infrequently." [11]

If you are in a minority culture, you might feel that those in the dominant culture do not really understand you. You don't know if you fit in, or if the members of the dominant culture expect you to perform, think, emote and react as they would. In a conversation about the differences in how employees learn a new system, an employee of a large company said, "There are several reasons why Hispanics might have difficulty in learning the system. Typically, these individuals do not come from the center of the universe. For example, Puerto Rico is not exactly the center. American kids, on the other hand, think they are the center and that they can make things happen. Also, the typical Hispanic attitude is not congruent with the system. For example, the system responds to my thinking that it is up to me to do it. The Hispanic culture suggests that it is up to us to do it."[12]

Most every organization's attempt at becoming culturally diverse includes stories of misunderstandings. This is especially evident in issues of power. In a discussion in *Christianity Today* on multicultural churches, pastor Soong-Chan Rah said, "I think with whites, laying down power comes down to a willingness to be in submission to those outside their community." The response of a prominent pastor also participating in the discussion reveals how differently the two view power: "I think the way a Caucasian hears the power question is a little different. It has been a turnoff to me, because the language doesn't line up with our core values at [his church]. Besides redemption itself, our church's highest value is servanthood. It's never been about power. We've never recruited 'powerful' people. We've watched God raise up people who have powerful and anointed ministries because they were humble and willing servants. And so that's an issue that pushes my buttons."[13]

Those who are in power tend to think of it as this pastor did. Because they have power, it is easy to misunderstand its importance and its use. Those who do not have power see it as Soong-Chan Rah did.

Dominant culture is more than skin color; it is also shared experiences, beliefs, values and behaviors. If someone came to your church and questioned a core teaching, such as infant baptism, that person would probably not be given much space to influence church matters. A dominant culture doesn't readily see power inequities. Neither does it want to relinquish power, since it has thrived precisely because it has a dominant position. The greater the distance between two cultures, the more difficult it is for the nondominant culture to influence the other group.

EXTROVERSION/INTROVERSION

As an introvert, I never cease to be amazed at how easily extroverts start and maintain conversations with perfect strangers. For most extroverts, everyone is a potential friend. Extroverts process information through engagement. When interacting with others, extroverts experience a feeling of elation and energy. Therefore, extroverts walk into a room with a stronger presence. They are anticipating the chance to visit, exchange ideas and be energized by people time. Introverts, on the other hand, process information internally. Their energy is renewed by introspection and reflection. Introverts walk into a room knowing that even though it might be a pleasant experience, they will be drained by the time it ends. Unless introverts learn how to "turn on" their presence, they usually take up less social space.

AGE

For one class that I taught, I divided the students by gender and talked to each group separately. I asked them what were the particular challenges they faced as leaders. The men talked about leadership and relationship concerns. The women did too, but they also talked about something else—age. The group ranged in age from mid-twenties to early sixties. The younger women were energetic and excited about their leadership roles and future possibilities. The older women had less enthusiasm. They were beginning to feel more and more invisible as leaders, as if they were no longer relevant. In our culture, ageism is "systematic," especially for women.[14]

It's no secret that Western culture is infatuated with youth. I try not to be influenced by it, but as I age I admit that I feel the pressure. Men feel it too, as they are going in increasing numbers to get face lifts and hair treatments for balding. Americans spend billions on cosmetic surgeries, spas, face creams and diets, trying to reverse the effects of time. In 2005 alone Americans spent almost $12.4 billion on cosmetic procedures.[15] Being older in our culture is less than advantageous. It is not uncommon for the elderly to be overlooked and go unnoticed. Toni Calasanti called it "the quest to be not old."[16] When it comes to power and influence, most Westerners instinctively understand that youthfulness in appearance, or at least in attitude, is preferred. Because males are usually given more power, an older male is still given more respect more than an older female. The older man is seen as having experience and wisdom, but the older woman is seen as less relevant.

PHYSICAL FEATURES

After I gave a presentation on power and presence at a conference for a large, respected parachurch organization, a man approached me to talk. He said he believed that he wasn't advancing as a leader because he was short. I was reticent to encourage this line of thinking, but he went on to make his case. Although he shared the same leadership experience as others, whenever an opportunity for advancement came up, a taller colleague was always chosen instead of him. I still wasn't convinced, but then he pointed out all the top leaders at the conference—and every one of them was quite tall. This man's experience doesn't mean that height is a predictor of success, as illustrated by the denomination superintendent in chapter five, but it does seem to help.

I have a nephew who is strikingly handsome. He is tall, athletic, and has dark, wavy hair and strong masculine features. He also has an easy, laid-back presence, which makes him approachable. Whenever he goes somewhere, he is noticed and watched. Fortunately, he doesn't seem to notice or care much himself, but the fact is, good looks equal greater attention. Good looks also breed an inner confidence that impacts a person's comfort level in social settings. People with ordinary features or those who are overweight or excessively thin do not get the same recognition, nor do they usually have the same confidence. It's not very common to find overweight people in significant leadership roles.

For women especially, physical features are a central part of their identity in this body- and beauty-obsessed culture. The perfect beauty is shapely but thin, young and pretty. Attractive women get noticed more and are treated differently than ordinary-looking women. I have observed this over and over again. If an attractive woman asks a man a question, she usually gets a warmer and more attentive response than an unattractive woman does. Women may be discriminated against in the workplace both for being too pretty or not pretty enough. A woman who is too beautiful might not be taken seriously as a leader. On the other hand, Naomi Wolf documents in her book *The Beauty Myth* cases of women who were fired for homeliness.[17] It becomes a Catch-22, especially for women who want to make a difference.

ECONOMIC AND SOCIAL STATUS

During a break at a pastor's conference, I joined a group of other attendees to discuss the speaker's main points. Over the course of our ten-minute discussion, one person mentioned the names of three nationally known Christian leaders, referring to them as personal friends. We've all been around name-droppers, and we often feel tempted to do the same. It can be a thrill to talk to or be close to someone who is wealthy or famous. Having economic status or fame, or being connected to it, brings prestige. Prestige equals presence and the power that goes with it. A well-known author, preacher or public figure turns heads, and others give that person more respect than may be wise without the presence of other qualities.

Churches often give the highest leadership positions to those who have prestigious jobs in the secular world. We often conclude that a wealthy man or woman is a successful man or woman. We assume that if they are successful with money, they must be successful in other parts of life. Some churches even equate economic success with God's favor. We are impressed with economic status, especially if it comes with fame. Wealthy and famous people take up more social space than the disadvantaged. Persons of lower status keep a greater physical and psychological distance between themselves and those of higher status because they are afraid of being judged, ridiculed or negatively assessed.[18]

STYLE OF DRESS

In the early eighties, my family and I returned to the United States after working in the Andes Mountains of Peru and Bolivia for several years. It was the end of the summer, and a recession was in full swing. My husband, Randy, applied everywhere for a job, but he couldn't get one. He often got to the interview level but was never hired. By December our savings was nearly gone, and we were getting anxious. Randy decided to do something out of character for him—he went out and bought a new, contemporary suit, shelling out a couple hundred dollars in the process. At his next job interview, dressed in his new suit, he was offered the job. We do not think that was coincidental.

Clothes broadcast a person's self-perception and self-identity. People can use distinctive clothes to set themselves apart or make a statement about their social status. Couture designer labels and conspicuous jewelry are used to make an impression. Conversely, people who don't want to make an impression or who are low-ranking members of a particular group will dress inconspicuously to hide or protect themselves.[19]

An individual's freedom to interact, to be noticed and heard, is often affected by the way a person dresses. Teenagers understand this explicitly. Establishing identity in their world is often determined by the clothes they wear and their comfort level in wearing them. Wearing the right clothes is not enough. The clothes and the body become a complete package that says something—a lot in fact—about the wearer. When Dale Chihuly, a well-known artist, received an honorary doctorate from Gonzaga University in 1996, he wore the required academic garb for the occasion, but he also wore bright red tennis shoes. The audience couldn't miss them as he processed to the distinguished guests' platform. Apparently the academic style of dress did not suit his style, so he accessorized to make it his own.

EDUCATION

I have been in situations where I was virtually ignored until people discovered that I have a Ph.D. and teach at a seminary. Although I am the same person postdoctorate as I was predoctorate, I am often surprised that I am received much more seriously now. When I give a presentation, I know that others will at least be curious about what I have to say because I have a doctorate. Otherwise, as a woman in a leadership environment dominated by males, I am often invisible. My husband, on the other hand, has an impressive appearance with distinguished white hair, nice-looking features and tall stature. When he walks into a room "duded up," as I like to say, people notice him and address him. When we are introduced to others, people usually assume that he is the one with the doctorate.

Education makes a difference in how seriously other people take you. We value knowledge and information. On the other hand, some faith traditions are suspect of education. These groups place greater value on other types of life experience, such as the evidence of spiritual gifts. All social groups value some type of knowledge or life experience that gives certain individuals more authority than others.

MARITAL STATUS

Many people believe the church is geared toward married people. Programs, sermons and special events often focus on couples or families. The highest positions of influence in a church are rarely given to single people. A pastor who is unmarried is seen as a liability (unless of course he's a Catholic priest). The larger the church, the less likely it is for the pastor to be single. I know a woman who had copastored a church with her husband for years, and then she was dismissed after her husband's death. Even though she had two children at home, the church said they wanted someone who was married so they could focus on family ministry. This woman's singleness, though unwanted and unchosen, was seen as a liability for that church.

Some believe it is unbiblical not to marry. A website promoting biblical manhood and womanhood takes a look at this issue from a different perspective:

> Today's singleness is not celibacy-induced kingdom work unaccommodating to family life. No, it's the result of choices and mistakes by both the individual and society. Today's singleness is either a lifestyle option or purely circumstantial; therefore, it is largely unbiblical. . . . We are a generation that blinds itself to the notion that the failure to marry timely (i.e., in the Spring of our adult lives) can be as costly as a divorce. It costs someone a spouse, it robs someone of legitimate sexual relations, it deprives grandparents of their grandchildren, it fails to replenish the nursery of the church.[20]

Though we may not consciously agree with the author's conclusions, our culture still tends to give more power to married people. Single men and single women both attest to the pressure they get from family, friends and the church to marry. Marriage is seen as normative, and singleness, abnormal.

ROLE AUTHORITY

As covered in chapter two, various roles entail varying levels of power and authority. Based on first impressions, a group gives a person with role authority more influencing space than those without. The pastor gets more attention than the usher. The company president has more influencing space than the administrative assistant. Roles are also represented by the arrangement of physical space. Large corner offices with imposing desks are reserved for the people with the most important roles in the organization. Uniforms, workspace size, and greeting and introduction rituals are all used to establish role authority and thus formalize the relationship. The more formalized the rituals that represent a person's role, the more power he or she has to influence. The more formalized the role authority, the greater the physical distance that is kept from others. For example, Britain's Queen Elizabeth is not to be touched. Several years ago an international uproar occurred when a gracious African American woman gave the queen a big hug when she was visiting in New York.

CONFIDENCE IN CHRIST

The interpretation of character was a special interest of the ancient Greeks and Romans, who made a science of studying the physical body and correlating values to certain features. They examined the body and the emotions that registered on a person's face, especially in the appearance of the eyes. This type of study is called physiognomics, and Hippocrates, the father of medicine, established it as a science.[21] Aristotle developed the first systematic usage of it. He believed that character was affected by the body, and the body responds to the nature of the soul. Aristotle (or his students) classified types of noses: high, curved noses indicated lustfulness; bulbous noses, insensitivity; slender, hooked noses displayed nobility. This ancient study was popular through the nineteenth century. Though today we do not promote the "science" of equating physical features with character qualities, we still unconsciously make value judgments about a person's place in a group by such visual cues. We decide whether or not a person can influence us.

Many religious leaders judged Jesus for his lack of qualifications. To them, he was the illegitimate son of a working-class man. He had nothing to offer them. Instead, they considered him a threat. The apostle Paul, on the other hand, had the highest credentials, but he did not put his confidence in them or value them highly, as he wrote in Philippians 3:4-9:

> I, too, have reason for confidence in the flesh. If anyone else has reason to be confident in the flesh, I have more: circumcised on the eighth day, a member of the people of Israel, of the tribe of Benjamin, a Hebrew born of Hebrews; as to the law, a Pharisee; as to zeal, a persecutor of the church; as to righteousness under the law, blameless. Yet whatever gains I had, these I have come to regard as loss because of Christ. More than that, I regard everything as loss because of the surpassing value of knowing Christ Jesus my Lord. For his sake I have suffered the loss of all things, and I regard them as rubbish, in order that I may gain Christ and be found in him, not having a righteousness of my own that comes from the law, but one that comes through faith in Christ.

This chapter is not intended to build "confidence in the flesh"; our only authentic confidence is in Christ. But, like Paul, awareness of the flesh helps us understand how it can be a conduit for God's purposes. For example, Paul used his status as a Roman citizen in to avoid a flogging and imprisonment (Acts 22:25-29). The difficulty for us is that our visual interpretations are where our fallenness is most visible. We are more impressed and do give more influence to people who have these visual markers. They have more presence because they are given more presence. They have more influence because they are given more influence. In the next chapter, we move on to second impressions, the visceral markers, which further define a group's pecking order.

QUESTIONS FOR DISCUSSION

1. Evaluate your presence in a particular ministry setting, such as a church meeting, staff meeting or small group. Which are your positive visuals that create space for you to influence, and which visual markers make you invisible? How would you describe your presence overall?

2. Have you ever experienced culture shock? Why is it so disorienting? How might your culture be disorienting for outsiders? How does culture impact your presence in a group where you are the outsider?

3. Which of the visual markers have you used to evaluate a new person who enters one of your social settings?

4. Think of a group to which you belong. Who has the most presence? Who has the least?

7

SECOND IMPRESSIONS

Visceral Marks of Presence

**Because of this many of his disciples turned
back and no longer went about with him.**
JOHN 6:66

Recently I was invited to a special conference for Christian leaders
sponsored by Leadership Network, a group whose mission it is "to
identify, connect and help high-capacity Christian leaders multiply
their impact." Prior to the conference, Leadership Network distributed pictures of the leaders invited to the conference, along with a
list of their accomplishments. These were all seasoned leaders. After
reviewing the list, I immediately had some first impressions about
which leaders I wanted to meet. A few were not as interesting to
me—frankly, I am ashamed to say, because of assumptions I made
about their theology. On the first day of the conference, after initial
introductions we were split up into pairs to share stories of recent
leadership struggles. I ended up with one of the people I hadn't been
interested in, but after she told her story to me, my first impression
was dramatically changed. In fact, we are friends today.

We often use internal filters to assess whether a person we are meeting for the first time is safe and whether the relationship could hurt or enhance our position in a group. The first layer of filters are the first impressions, the visuals, which we discussed in the previous chapter. The next layer of filters, the second impressions, are also instinctual and quickly formed. I call them the viscerals. Malcolm Gladwell in *Blink* used research in neuroscience and psychology to demonstrate that people who most often make good decisions focus on a few specific details.[1] Visceral markers are those details that we use to decide whether or not we will trust someone. Viscerals are more difficult to define, and they are more complex.

With second impressions, a variety of things can occur. A person may be confirmed in the amount of space they have already been given, whether it is a little or a lot. Or a person may be given more or less influencing credibility than the first impressions indicated. In other words, second impressions confirm, enhance or reduce a person's influencing space. If he or she is given more, a tentative trust is established. Sometimes the qualities that produce a favorable first impression (the visuals) are not present, but the qualities that produce second impressions (the viscerals) might be significant, especially when several of them are packaged together. This is why Mother Teresa was such a potent force for the poor. A first impression showed a form and attire that were quite humble, but second impressions, such as her godly character and spirit, were often referred to in glowing terms by those who met her.

In social settings, people generally behave in ways based on their interpretation of their own visual presence. A woman on a ministry team spoke very little because she didn't have the seminary education that the others had. She was intimidated and thought it would be best to stay quiet. A young Asian man serving on a worship team constantly discarded his own ideas. He struggled with the perception that his youthfulness disqualified him from contributing. When a person self-identifies based on superficial visual markers, the power of second impressions, the viscerals, is less likely to be tapped and developed. Figure 5 lists some visceral markers that may contribute to more or less presence.

More Presence	Less Presence
Focused; purposeful	Unfocused
Taking risks	Avoiding risks
Optimistic; hopeful	Depressed; cynical
Gifts of leadership and charisma	Gifts of serving and mercy
Defined boundaries	Fuzzy or no boundaries
High social interaction	Low social interaction
Making eye contact	Avoiding eye contact
Using appropriate touch	Avoiding touch

Figure 5.

FOCUS

Janis Miglavs, a former *National Geographic* photojournalist, has a passion to photograph and record the cultural myths and dreams of the shamans, elders and chiefs of hidden and disappearing tribes. He has dedicated his life and resources to capturing their stories in images before they are lost. He travels all over the world to remote and dangerous places, and he seems unafraid. When people like Janis feel they have a purpose in life and work to accomplish it, they are not intimidated by difficult circumstances or powerful people. Focused people are willing to approach others, no matter who they are, if it means reaching their goals. They are persistent. Those with a sense of personal destiny and purpose seek the best ways to reach their objectives. They don't worry about whether they have the right to barge into another person's busy life.

Owen and Sandie Brock of the Servants, a hippie Christian rock band of the sixties and seventies, believed that Jesus would return soon. They and many others living in Southern California were miraculously healed of their drug addictions and destructive lifestyles by the Holy Spirit. That outpouring of the Holy Spirit caused them to believe that the second coming was imminent. Because of their expectation and their focus, the Brocks and their followers chose to imitate the early church. They lived in community and committed their lives to spreading the good news. Rather than preaching on street corners, they were one of the first groups to use drama and music to gather a crowd. Over the next ten years, they did not falter in their belief that Jesus was on the fast track to return. That focus defined their lives and gave them the courage to use music and drama when no one else had a vision for the power of the arts to bring people to Christ. When it became clear that Jesus would not return as soon as they expected, they redefined their mission and invited struggling young men and women to live in community with them until they got back on their feet.

A sense of direction clarifies life. It narrows down a myriad of possibilities to one clear path. The extraordinary success of Rick Warren's book and message *The Purpose-Driven Life* testifies to our need for purpose. When we know our purpose, hardships, suffering, lack of resources, gender and race all fall away. With purpose comes clarity, and then nothing can get in the way of pursuing that God-breathed passion. Those who have this intense focus are comfortable taking up space in social settings.

RISK

I enjoy watching athletes because the best ones continually hone their skills and take risks. The Iron Man World Triathlon and the Olympics—in fact, most sporting events—are inspiring to watch precisely because people are doing their competitive best and persevering in the face of great risk. Bethany Hamilton was an elite surf-boarder who was attacked by a fourteen-foot tiger shark off Kauai's North Shore at the age of thirteen. The shark took off her left arm. Three months later, Bethany returned to the competitive circuit, and five months after that, she placed fifth at the National Scholastic Surfing Association championships.

Risk-taking is not just an athletic feat. People take risks in planting a new church, starting a creative social program, moving overseas to be neighbors with strangers or opening a new business or art studio. Jesus often took risks, whether healing on the sabbath or challenging the Pharisees' motives for tithing. Those who are comfortable taking risks take up more social space. People who are averse to taking risks rarely say or do anything to rock the boat. Risk-avoiders prefer the status quo out of fear that things might go terribly wrong. Risk-takers generally have more presence and more influence.

ATTITUDE

In a research study of the relationship between optimism and job success, Martin Seligman[2] tested fifteen thousand applicants for positions as life insurance sales reps. Selling life insurance is a difficult profession with a high drop-out rate because of the constant rejection in that line of work. Seligman measured levels of optimism and pessimism in qualified candidates. In his study, he also included a third group of 129 individuals who had failed the industry's hiring exams but who scored very high on the optimism profile. These individuals were hired anyway. After two years, optimists had outsold pessimists by a large margin, and the group of highest-scoring optimists, who had initially failed the industry's exams, outsold everyone.[3]

Optimism and hope are infectious. Cynicism and depression are not. Those who struggle with depression find it difficult to be fully present in social settings. Their feelings are usually flat, and the smallest social interaction is taxing. Depressed people withdraw.

They may become lost in their despair and be less aware of their social environment. Depression shows on a person's face; it is not open and engaged. Even if members of a group are compassionate, they rarely give a depressed or cynical person leadership space.

BOUNDARIES

A friend shared with me the following story about two friends, both pastors:

> My friend Brian works sixty to seventy hours a week. He is involved in almost every meeting and function. He takes part in many programs in his community. I have called the church office at various times of the day, on various days of the week, and he's almost always there or in a meeting and expected back soon. I participated in a Habitat for Humanity building project last summer with his church, and Brian was there early. He brought watermelon. He led a work crew, played his guitar and led singing. And even though the temperature was near one hundred degrees, he didn't take a single break all day. On Sundays Brian appears scattered. I do not see him as often as I would like, but when I do, his mind is going a hundred miles an hour. His eyes often shift back and forth, looking for the next person to talk to and the next task to accomplish. Parishioners often wonder if he is really listening when they talk to him.
>
> My other friend, Tom, takes every Monday off and allows no interruptions. This is his Sabbath. On Tuesdays he is available at home if he's needed for emergencies. He works the rest of the week but only stays in the office until noon. Committees, task forces, informal worship and many programs happen without him. He is involved in the community, but not to the extent that he is overcommitted. On Sundays Tom is calm and collected. He takes time to engage with and focus on each indi-

vidual he encounters. He laughs and jokes with members and friends. He listens.

Brian and Tom give two different visceral experiences in social space. One is scattered; the other, relaxed. Brian had a problem with boundaries. He was consumed by his job. Having boundaries means knowing where the "I" begins and ends in relationship to work or to other people:

> This sense of separateness forms the basis of personal identity. It says what we are and what we are not, what we will choose and what we will not choose, what we will endure and what we will not, what we feel and what we will not feel, what we like and what we do not like, and what we want and what we do not want. Boundaries, in short, define us.[4]

Defined boundaries help everyone feel safe. Research shows that people with more definite boundaries exhibit more socially engaging behaviors such as being active, assertive and communicative in interpersonal relationships. They listen better. Brian did not separate his ministry from his identity. Tom did.

There are different types of boundary problems. While Brian's had to do with his job, others have trouble separating themselves from individuals. This usually happens because they were not encouraged or allowed to develop a sense of self apart from someone else. Overbearing or needy parents sometimes treat their children as an extension of themselves. The child doesn't know where he or she begins and the parent ends. This carries over into an adulthood in which boundaries are fuzzy. These people are easily confused about what they want and what is appropriate. They tend to be more passive and withdrawn in their behaviors.

Self-identity and self-esteem are reflected in one's ability to keep healthy spatial boundaries in a group. People with healthy boundaries instinctively understand that an invasion of their personal space, whether physical or emotional, is an affront to their personhood. If the boundaries are too permeable, the person may not be able to maintain a clear sense of self, or they may feel so insecure that others easily override them. As a result, those without boundaries are not given much power.

SOCIAL INTERACTION

Lisa, an acquaintance, shared that she grew up in a home with a domineering and competitive father. He constantly pushed his kids to achieve, and he created and thrived on a loud, aggressive home environment. Lisa's reaction was insecurity and withdrawal. Near the end of her sophomore year in high school, Lisa's dad announced they'd be moving to another state that summer. Lisa decided to make a fresh start as a junior at her new school. She began observing the popular girls. She noticed that in the bathroom they spent time looking directly at their reflection in the mirror, confidently fixing their hair or putting on makeup. By the time Lisa arrived at her new school, she'd decided on two deliberate changes in her behavior. First, she would walk up to other students and say, "Hi, I'm Lisa. I'm new here." And second, whenever she went in the girls' bathroom, she would go to the mirror, look directly at herself, primp and fix her hair. Now an adult, Lisa reflected, "It's almost scary how completely the popular kids accepted me into the inner circle and my life changed."

Social interaction is a learned behavior. Learning social skills leads to more self-confidence. Increased confidence results in more presence and influence. Lisa taught herself the social cues that could move her from a shy, insecure person to a confident, interactive one, and as a result, she changed her status. As adults, our interests should go beyond popularity to things such as increased effectiveness. High social interactors know the basic skills they need to interact appropriately with anyone they might meet. They know social graces that allow them to walk up to a stranger, introduce themselves and initiate an engaging conversation. I have seen plain and ordinary people light up a room by drawing others into conversations. High social interactors create a spirit of hospitality. Their priorities are getting to know others and helping them feel comfortable and accepted.

Social interaction is distinct from the personality characteristics of extroversion and introversion. An extrovert might be clueless about the social cues inundating him or her, and vice versa, an introvert can learn to be a high social interactor. My first-grade teacher wrote in my report card, "She is overly shy, withdrawn and average in intelligence." I was a timid and insecure little girl. As a teenager I was unsure how to talk with people or how to act around others. But today, few people would guess that I was once withdrawn. I am still an introvert, but I have learned the art of being "on deck" in social settings.

In the movie *My Fair Lady,* snobbish linguist professor Henry Higgins successfully transforms a flower street vendor, Eliza Doolittle, into a refined woman. Like Ms. Doolittle (perhaps with a bit less singing), anyone can learn the skills to take command of a social setting. The best way to learn social skills, such as appropriate eye contact, body position and touch, is to observe and imitate the people who have them.

EYE CONTACT AND BODY POSITION

One of the first lessons I learned during my process of becoming a better social interactor was how to make eye contact when meeting people. It sounds like such a simple skill, but it's surprising how seldom people use it. Before, I would look down or away or shift my eyes. I felt uncomfortable with direct eye contact. But I was unintentionally communicating vulnerability and lack of confidence, so I had to get over it. In Western culture, direct eye contact is necessary in order to be an influencer. In most Asian cultures the opposite is

true. The proper downward gaze shows respect. American politicians, who are dependent on voters to get into office, look directly at
the people they are meeting. Direct eye contact communicates "I'm
interested in you." It can also indicate authority. When a boss looks
someone directly in the eye, it says, "I have more power than you
do." An unwavering look asserts dominance.

Eye contact is intense. A person does not usually gaze into someone else's eyes for more than three seconds. Eye contact is minimal
with a person who is disliked. In a group setting, the amount of
eye contact individuals make and the amount they receive is a good
indicator of their level of influence. Eye contact also affects body
position. Where the eye goes, the body goes. Wherever a person is
looking, his or her body will orient in that direction, and body orientation reflects status in a group. The more influence and status a
person has, the more likely it is that others in the group will orient
their bodies toward that individual. The less status a person has, the
more likely it is that group members, especially women, will orient
their bodies away from the individual.

TOUCH

Experts on touch analyzed a forty-one-minute video of a Senate floor
vote and found that senators match the body language of their opponent. They also use touch to assert power or to bond.[5] Touch is a
powerful communicator. Intentional touching moves an interaction
from public space to social, personal or intimate space. Throughout
the world, touch is used to express emotion, especially in the process
of establishing rapport, in courting rituals and in offering comfort.
Using touch to show affection to children is also normative across
cultures, but the amount of touching adults do in public varies from
culture to culture. For instance, one research study that analyzed
adolescents eating together in McDonald's restaurants found that
teens in Paris touched more frequently than their peers in Miami.[6]

In Western culture, warm handshakes and brief hugs establish rapport in a group. When women use a firm handshake, they are perceived as being smart and willing to take risks.[7] A handshake can convey more intimacy than is warranted if one person takes the other's hand in both of their own. A hug conveys acceptance and excitement at being together. Touch can also establish dominance, such as when a person with more authority touches someone with less. For example, if a counselor touches the knee of a patient during a session in his or her office, it is intimidating and inappropriate. On the other hand, if a person avoids touch, others are less likely to initiate and sustain a relationship with him or her.

THE DARK SIDE OF PRESENCE

Not all leaders who have presence and take up a lot of social space are emotionally and spiritually healthy. It would be naive to conclude that just because a person has focus, social skills, leadership gifts or any other of the visceral markers that they can be trusted with power. Presence is not automatically innocent. People can project a façade of servant leadership. Some leaders are adored in public, but behind closed doors they are more than difficult to be around. And some of these leaders are not just having a bad day. They are unaware, or choose to ignore, the dark side of their own presence. In *Overcoming the Dark Side of Leadership,* Gary McIntosh and Sam Rima present various dysfunctions commonly found in leaders.[8] In fact, they argue that the very nature of leadership often attracts unhealthy individuals. Some of these leaders take up a great deal of social space but exude a false confidence.

Listed below are the most common dysfunctions of leaders. I've divided the unhealthy characteristics into two categories: the ones that create more presence and the ones that contribute to less. Note that each marker can range from mildly to severely unhealthy, from unhealthy coping mechanisms to full-blown personality disorders, which only a qualified therapist or psychologist can diagnose.

Narcissism and histrionics. Narcissistic and histrionic personalities need a great deal of social space. They often have a flamboyant presence. Their hidden insecurities drive them to do things so they

Unhealthy, Creating More Presence	Unhealthy, Contributing to Less Presence
Narcissism and histrionics	Dependent personality
Rebel stance	Passive stance
Authoritarianism	Submissiveness

Figure 6.

are noticed, listened to and set apart as special. Because of these internal drives, they often seek high-profile roles. Characteristics of narcissists include grandiosity, entitlement, arrogance and a need to dominate and control. They do not easily empathize with others, so they may be unaware of or unable to take into consideration another person's ideas and feelings. They often claim a good idea as their own, even if it originated with someone else. To feel important, they may create chaos by disagreeing or setting up roadblocks to remain in control. Narcissists also engage in magical thinking, making ideas and situations seem more perfect and wonderful than they really are. This causes them to exaggerate their capacities and potentials.

Histrionic personalities are characterized by a constant need to create drama through excessive emotional displays, sexual seductiveness or attention-seeking behaviors. These people are not as likely to be found in Christian leadership roles because they are usually female and their sexual behavior makes them an uncomfortable fit in a religious environment. However, those with milder histrionic tendencies may be found in leadership in any setting. Both histrionic and narcissistic individuals take up a lot of social space with their need to be the center of attention.

Rebel stance and passive stance. A healthy dose of rebellion, such as resisting evil or injustice, can be positive depending on the circumstances, motivations and manner in which it is applied. But when someone adopts a rebel stance to feel unique or special, it is unhealthy and counterproductive. It can be a cover-up for insecurities or reactions to past hurts. Leaders with a rebel stance pride themselves on being edgy and outside the box. They can take up a lot of space in a social setting trying to prove themselves and the rightness of their cause. On the other hand, anxiety-prone individuals maintain greater distances from others. Those who are withdrawn and passive are unable to engage competently in group processes.

Authoritarianism and submissiveness. Authoritarian leaders generally have low self-esteem. They are characterized by rigidity and conventionalism or traditionalism. Highly authoritarian individuals take up a lot of social space, especially if they perceive a threat to their status, values and way of life. When threatened, they can become more aggressive. They can be very intimidating, especially if they have role power. Authoritarian leaders keep themselves safe and protect their egos through verbal or physical aggression.

Submissive individuals are the polar opposite of authoritarians. They are characterized by the need to defer to others and to remain in a powerless relationship with others. They rarely become leaders unless assigned role power by an authoritarian leader who wants a person who will submit to his or her will. The submissive leader's insecurity is protected by taking up as little space as possible and keeping connected to the person in power who will protect him or her.

There are other types of unhealthy leaders, but the narcissist, histrionic, rebel and authoritarian are the four that are particularly noticeable in social space. They use presence in unhealthy and intimidating ways to influence others according to their predetermined will. Even though a group usually has the choice of whether or not to give such a person space to influence, unfortunately most groups don't have the training or tools to effectively handle an unhealthy leader.

PRESENCE AND EMOTIONAL-SPIRITUAL HEALTH

Emotional and spiritual health may be personal realities, but they are played like a brass band in relational settings: whether you are healthy or unhealthy, others will know. The closer the physical space—social, personal and intimate—the more is revealed of our inner selves. Rubbing shoulders with others brings out the best and the worst in us. Those with exceptional emotional and spiritual health are usually perceived by others as safe, and as a result are often given social space to influence. In the Quaker tradition, these are called "weighty Friends." Their spiritual and emotional wholeness carries weight in discernment processes. Most of us, though, are still on a journey toward the imago Dei. We have good days and bad days, healthy and unhealthy moments. However, the healthier we are, the more aware we are of the complexity of our inner world and the more able we are to discern Christlike thoughts, emotions and behaviors from the un-Christlike.

In church and ministry settings, the use of social space is a barometer indicating the health of the group and the individuals in the group. A healthy group trusts and collaborates with each other. There is a level of intimacy and camaraderie shared around common purposes. We can improve our own individual and group emotional-spiritual health by observing how our bodies instinctually interact. Some people find this difficult because they don't read social cues very well. An inability to see beneath the skin and interpret the relational interactions between people is considered a lack of emotional intelligence.[9] Learning about the visual and visceral markers helps us observe and talk about those things that are difficult to infer. Being aware of and thinking about the dynamics of presence in a social setting guards the individuals and the group from making assumptions about who has influence and who does not.

Assumptions are a handicap because they prevent us from seeing and evaluating the use of power. Awareness leads us to think about presence in a group. If you are aware of what you bring visually and viscerally into a group, and the amount of presence these markers generate, you can be more proactive in improving or moderating the use of influence and power. If the group as a whole is aware, the members can begin to discuss it. Awareness triggers a group's capacity to be Christlike. Everyone in the body takes responsibility for understanding his or her presence so that the power to influence belongs to the whole.

QUESTIONS FOR DISCUSSION

1. Using the same ministry setting you shared in chapter six, evaluate your presence in light of your visceral markers. Which ones are positive and create space for you to influence, and which ones keep you invisible? How would you describe your presence now?

2. Have you been in a group with unhealthy individuals who took up a lot of social space? How did the group handle it?

3. Think of a particular group to which you belong. Who in the group has the most presence? Who has the least? Has the group ever talked about it? Can the group talk about it?

4. Are there other visceral markers that you use to determine who has presence and who does not? Are there other cultural characteristics that you or your group use to determine whether someone is accepted or given influence?

8

BEAN-COUNTING SOCIAL SPACE
The Economics of Power

I need more space.

JULIA ROBERTS, ON PURCHASING
THIRTY-TWO ACRES IN NEW MEXICO

[Leighton] Ford is now "simply walking in
people's souls" and finding out what God
is doing there. . . . "He may spend the rest
of his life working primarily with 10 people.
. . . It might not be on a grand scale, but the
impact could be exponential."

LAUREN WINNER

When we walk into a room, the visuals and viscerals of our presence
are quickly calculated by members of the group as they figure the
amount of influence they will give us. The processes of addition and
subtraction are continually active. We all do this in social settings.
We make snap decisions about whether newcomers are safe and can

be trusted with who we are and what we're about. These decisions have sticking power; once they're made, they're hard to change.

Each of us is given a measure of power. There is a steady exchange of power potential negotiated within groups. Like dance partners, we move in social space exchanging meaning in a quiet rhythm of relational cues and discernment. Some people are given more power and some less, but everyone is involved. Power doesn't belong to any one person—it belongs to the group that constitutes it. The exception is when force is used to make the group follow the will of the leader. So the use of power is not just a moral issue, as we discussed in chapter two; it is also a stewardship issue. God called us to steward the resources of his creation, and I suggest that power is one of those resources. The acquisition, management, consumption and distribution of resources are economic issues. So also are the acquisition, management, use and distribution of power for equipping people to do the work of God's kingdom. Anyone who has an interest can learn to understand the economics of the forestry industry or small business. But how can we understand and manage the economics of power?

Even though we value servant leadership, which has a lot to do with the use of power, we usually aren't mindful of the stewardship of power. We tend to equate servant leadership with spiritual, internal character qualities manifested in a leader's public behaviors. However, authentic servant leadership involves stewardship of power, power used thoughtfully for God's purposes as an exchange within a group. It is a kind of bean-counting that acknowledges that gestures, invitations and "time attended to" all add up and matter. What a leader brings into a social space plus what happens between people in that space results in influence. Everything about the leader, from the first hello to the final decision, is a reflection of his or her stewardship of power—either for service or for personal gain.

THE STORY OF DR. LEIGHTON FORD

Leighton Ford is an impressive man. He is handsome, stands at six feet four with a trim build, and has distinguished gray hair. You can't miss him when he enters a room. He has a relaxed, open presence and great social skills. He'll walk up to anyone and begin a conversation. Dr. Ford seems genuinely interested in who you are and what you are about. People appreciate him for his warmth, sharp mind, thoughtful spirituality and creative gifts. He writes poems and paints watercolors, a true Renaissance man. Often when he speaks publicly, he'll quote an entire poem from memory.

A quick survey of Dr. Ford's life reflects the different realms in which he has power. For thirty years, he was both an evangelist and administrator for the Billy Graham Evangelistic Association, traveling worldwide and preaching the gospel to thousands. For sixteen years, he chaired the Lausanne Committee for World Evangelization. His book *Transforming Leadership: Jesus' Way of Creating Vision, Shaping Values and Empowering Change* is a classic among Christian leadership books. After his son Sandy died in 1981 at the age of twenty-one, Dr. Ford shifted the focus of his considerable leadership gifts to mentoring and training young leaders with a passion for evangelism.

Several years ago while I was working on my doctoral dissertation on Jesus and leadership, I read Dr. Ford's book on the topic. A few months later I attended a seminar where Dr. Ford was the speaker. After his presentation, I approached him with questions about the practicalities of leadership training and formation. After our conversation, he invited me to visit his Arrow Leadership Training program in Charlotte, North Carolina. I gladly accepted and went later that spring. I went as an observer to learn about leadership training. When I arrived, Dr. Ford himself picked me up for the two-hour drive to the retreat center where the training sessions were held. I had expected his assistant to pick me up or that I would ride with other attendees. I felt honored, and even more so when he said he wanted to get to know me. During the long drive, we had a stimulating conversation about leadership, our spiritual journeys and the challenges facing the next generation of leaders.

Later at the retreat center, I attended the evening banquet where young people from all over the world—some of the brightest entrepreneurial leaders I've ever met—were gathered. Before the meal, Dr. Ford introduced his guests. When it was my turn, he told the students a little about me and then said, "This is someone you must have a conversation with. She is insightful, wise and spiritually astute. Get your datebooks out and make sure you get a chance to talk with her." Once again, I felt honored. After the meal, many of these young leaders asked to meet with me. I had come as an unknown but left feeling well-known and included. To have a person of such caliber and influence as Dr. Ford publicly declare that I had value and something important to contribute made a big impact on me as a developing leader. He anointed my gifts, and he made me want to be that kind of leader. Dr. Ford used his power resources to extend the influence of others—not only mine but that of hundreds of other developing leaders.

A STORY OF ANOTHER INFLUENCER

A woman who is well-known for her influence among conservatives was interviewed not long ago by *The Today Show*'s Matt Lauer. She is an attractive woman with long, blond hair, and impeccably dressed. She is a best-selling author and writes a weekly column for conservatives about current politics. Her $1.5 million condo in New York and $1.8 million home in Florida give testimony to her financial success. She is also a Christian. On the social power scale, her resources are formidable. Like Dr. Ford, she has presence and power, but hers is of a different kind.

During the interview, she criticized some New Jersey widows who had banded together after their husbands were killed on 9/11. They had used their political clout to influence the U.S. government to create the 9/11 Commission and to make national security against future attacks a government priority. Lauer's guest called these widows "the Witches of East Brunswick" and said, "How do we know their husbands weren't planning to divorce these harpies? Now that their shelf life is dwindling, they'd better hurry up and appear in Playboy."[1]

This woman used her influencing platform and power resources to criticize other women with whom she did not agree. I don't take issue with her right to hold a contrary viewpoint, but I do take issue with her use of influence to attack others. After this interview her book sales increased, and she was spotlighted in major papers, talk shows and newscasts across the United States. Though I don't know the real reasons behind her words, I suspect this type of aggressive response can be partially attributed to a Western economic perspective about the use of one's power resources.

Here we will explore how our view of economics impacts how we use power. Our Western values of personal freedom, independence and self-sufficiency sometimes cause us to misuse the power we have. This happens because we think of power as a resource independently acquired by our own efforts, not as something socially constructed in a group or as the resource of a group. With this attitude, it is easier for a leader to use power without thinking much about its social impact. If power is viewed as an individually acquired resource, then we assume the use of it is also individual and personal. We aren't aware or don't think about how our bodies can be used to abuse or honor others. The stewardship of our resources and the discipline of paying attention to our presence in social space—bean-counting, in effect—leads us to use power in keeping with Jesus' model of servant leadership.

THE STEWARDSHIP OF RESOURCES IN SCRIPTURE

The stewardship of resources is a dominant theme in Scripture. There are many verses on material possessions and the use of wealth throughout the Bible. Craig Blomberg, a New Testament scholar at Denver Seminary, summarized these biblical themes:

- "Material possessions are a good gift from God meant for his people to enjoy."

- "Material possessions are simultaneously one of the primary means of turning human hearts away from God."

- "A necessary sign of a life in the process of being redeemed is that of transformation in the area of stewardship."

- "There are certain extremes of wealth and poverty which in and of themselves are intolerable."

- "Above all, the Bible's teaching about material possessions is inextricably intertwined with more 'spiritual' matters. No ungodly poor people are ever exalted as models for emulation. No godly rich people, who are generous and compassionate in the use of their wealth, are ever condemned."[2]

If we go a step further, we can conclude that the stewardship theme in Scripture is about more than material possessions. It also encompasses immaterial possessions, and power is one of them. If we use Blomberg's words as a lens for looking at the immaterial possession of power, we can make these points:

- Power is a good gift from God meant for us to exercise with joy.

- Power is also one of the primary means of turning human hearts away from God.

- A necessary sign of life in the process of being redeemed is that of transformation in the area of our stewardship of power.

- There are certain extremes of powerfulness and powerlessness that are intolerable.

- The Bible's teaching about power, especially as illustrated by the life of Jesus, is inextricably intertwined with spiritual matters.

Jesus did not spiritualize the economic realities of his day. He spent much time in his ministry addressing the economic concerns of his audience: paying taxes, inheritance problems, the wages of day laborers. Jesus equated the use of resources with the quality of a person's devotion to God. Jesus critiqued those who misused their power for personal gain. He disapproved of the ruling elite, the wealthy religious leaders, not because of their wealth but because their stewardship of it was contrary to God's economics. They used their wealth to enhance their power rather than to serve others. In contrast, Jesus used his actions, words and mannerisms to serve rather than to acquire. Jesus wanted to redeem fiscal economics and nonfiscal resources, and his perspective was embedded in the economics of his culture.

DIVERGENT ECONOMICS: LIMITED AND UNLIMITED GOODS

Since leadership is a physical experience that is mainly palpable in social space, our use of that space is an economic issue with moral implications for us as Christians. Looking at the economic differences between first-century Jewish culture and twenty-first-century Western culture demonstrates this idea. The point of this comparison is not to say that one is bad and the other good but to illustrate how different cultural perceptions directly impact our understanding of power and its use in social space.

Limited-goods culture. The first-century Mediterranean world was a peasant society, with about 90 percent of the populace living in small rural environments and the rest living in preindustrial cities. These cities were populated mainly by the cultural elites and the artisans and working classes who served them, and they were dependent on the smaller villages for resources. Jerusalem was such a city, inhabited by Roman soldiers, Herodian rulers and religious leaders like the priests and Sadducees. These elites wielded the power to exact taxes from and execute laws over the entire population.

In this culture, the masses largely viewed themselves as being in an interdependent relationship with the persons in power, who represented and preserved the primary values of the culture. Peasants accepted their lot as limited and fixed. They may not have liked it, but usually they did not imagine it possible to change their status. For instance, a boy growing up in a carpenter's shop in Nazareth would never imagine that he could become a priest or Sadducee because those positions were a birthright.

Palestine was a limited-goods culture.[3] There was only so many physical resources, such as land, produce, livestock and fish, to go around. Resources could be used up. If people increased their holdings, such as land or wealth, it could only mean that others would have less. Therefore, the responsible approach to life was not to improve one's social status by acquiring more prestige and goods but to preserve the honor and position one's family already had.

In a limited-goods culture, those who had more were responsible for sharing with those who had less. Those who had less were responsible for maintaining loyal and supportive relationships with those who looked out for them. In this culture, a symbiotic relationship existed between the peasants and their patrons in power. People depended on social ties to keep things balanced. The roles of patrons, kinship groups and neighbors assured that justice was carried out and that everyone was taken care of, no matter how impoverished. During the first century, the economic system had begun to break down. Most of the rich land owners moved to the cities and increased their coffers, at the expense of the tenants of the land. The material gain of the one group meant fewer resources were available for the other. In neglecting their responsibility as patrons, the wealthy further impoverished the farmers and laborers. The patron-peasant relationship went bust.

The limited-goods perspective influenced nonmaterial resources as well. Anything of value was seen through this economic lens. Jesus challenged the deterioration of the limited-goods economic system as it impacted all areas of life.[4] Among first-century Jews, honor had the highest social value and was the greatest social resource. God had called them to be a holy people, and their whole culture had evolved to lift up this value. Because it was a limited-goods culture, honor was limited too. If honor came into dispute, either the status quo would be affirmed or one person would go away with less, one with more. Honor was challenged in public, and only between males. Jesus challenged the traditional views of value and honor. He used public social events, especially meals, to redistribute power. Jesus ate with sinners, while holy people would not. For Jesus, honor was not related to his human birthright or social position but came through an inclusive hospitality, through inviting anyone who followed him or sought him to come to the table with him. Jesus challenged the notion that some are inherently excluded from the social table while others naturally have a place at the head of the table. Instead of honor being acquired through public law-keeping, it came through public response to love with gratitude and inclusion. In a limited-goods culture, the honorable response to others was hospitality—not only in one's home but in one's life. An example is the hospitality event in Simon's house discussed in chapter three.

Using the limited-goods lens of first-century economics, as Jesus modeled it, can give us a fresh understanding of the use of power in social space. If we think of power as a limited resource, that there is only so much of it in a group, then the stewardship of it matters more. Here's an illustration. Let's say that power takes the tangible form of apples. In a limited-goods economy, a group of twelve people has twenty-four apples. Two individuals in the group are in possession of twenty of the apples. Their responsibility is to make sure that everyone has enough. They become the hosts and extend hospitality to the others. They invite everyone to the table to eat. The purpose of their having more is that they preserve and care for everyone else in the group. It is their responsibility to make sure that no one goes hungry. Selling the apples or eating most of the apples themselves would be contrary to this economic system. The response of those who receive the distributed apples is gratefulness and loyalty.

Unlimited goods. In contrast to first-century Jewish economics, twenty-first-century Western culture, particularly the United States, is an unlimited-goods economy. There are plenty of resources to go around. The rich do not think that their coffers represent wealth garnered at the expense of others or that because they have more, others have less. Those with power in Western culture often believe their positions of influence resulted from individual capacity and smart networking. This view is why top corporate executives earn such huge salaries and are wooed with extravagant incentives to stay with their company. Power as a resource is all about individual skills. If power to influence is an individual resource, it has limitless potential. Let's use the apple analogy again. In an unlimited-goods culture, if a group of twelve has twenty-four apples and twenty of them belong to two people, those two believe they got their apples because of their own hard work and good fortune. They might share the apples, but they don't have to because the apples belong to them as individual owners, not to the group. The group members without apples feel they need to go outside the group to get some. The attitude of the apple holders is "There are apples everywhere, so go and get your own." This attitude reflects the economic perspective that resources are unlimited.

The unlimited-goods economic view impacts how we carry our bodies in social space. We tend to be unaware of how much space we take up because we believe there is plenty of room for everyone. Internationally, Americans are often characterized as loud and obnoxious—taking up social space. The expansiveness of American behavior is a reflection of the Western economic attitude of unlimited goods, which is reflected not only in the loudness of our presence but in our feelings of entitlement toward occupying social and physical space. Because we believe we have garnered resources with our own efforts, we think we are entitled to take up all the space we need. In an interview with Bernard-Henri Lévy about his book *American Vertigo,* the author said, "The obesity of the body is a metaphor of another obesity. There is a tendency in America to believe that the bigger the better for everything—for churches, cities, malls, companies, and campaign budgets. There's an idolatry of bigness."[5] Being loud is a physical manifestation of being insensitive about the use of physical space. It is also an assumption of entitlement toward social and economic freedom that misses the assumption's impact on others.

This "idolatry of bigness" originated in a noble ideal. Americans' highest value is individual freedom, quite different from the primary value of honor in the first-century Jewish culture. The value of individual freedom means that every American is entitled to life, liberty and the pursuit of happiness, and we have government protection of those hard-earned resources. The underlying assumption is that success is limited only by a person's lack of determination and hard work. The mark of individual freedom is the freedom to live and work where we want, to say what we want and to avoid any persons, places or things that we don't want. In short, freedom is a "lack of spatial restrictions."[6]

The problem with attaching freedom to the limitless use of space is that life is bounded in physical space. Planet Earth has limitations.

A room has walls. A business has limits, as does a church. All physical resources can be used up. Life is comprised of innumerable interactions within those spatial limits.[7] Therefore, interactions also use up space. Americans take for granted the use of space by neglecting its economic capacity. Japanese culture is considered a highly space-conscious one, and American culture, a space-insensitive one.[8] The exploration, settlement and development of the vast continental United States was a hallmark of the American spirit.[9] Unfortunately, today we are running out of free space: "The still-dominant impulse to define freedom spatially has collided with one hard fact: there is little space left for expansion."[10]

The unlimited-goods perspective pervades everything from the basic management of resources to the quantities of resources the United States consumes compared to other countries. This attitude leads to consumerism with an insatiable appetite. Rather than resources belonging to the community, they are there for personal consumption and enjoyment. Rather than sharing, we go shopping. This attitude also impacts Western thinking about power and influence. Power and influence are seen as unlimited. So an individual can use his or her power whenever and in whatever way he or she sees fit, as long as it is legal and doesn't infringe on the basic value of freedom. There is little attentiveness to the impact of an individual's power in a group.

STEWARDSHIP AND POWER

These two divergent economic perspectives illustrate the different use of power in social space. The Western unlimited-goods perspective often results in wealthy and influential persons using large amounts of physical and social space. The use of physical space is symbolized by large homes and properties, huge walk-in closets, private jets, etc. The use of social space is symbolized by the larger-than-life presence that most influential persons are given in social space. Persons with the most social power are given the most social space. In a limited-goods culture, resources are scarce so people depend instead on social ties for security. Thus a poor person is not someone without material wealth but someone without a social network. A poor person is powerless because he or she is without a family or a patron. People are empowered to thrive when they belong to a family group with patrons. Instead of consumerism, which is considered dishonorable and immoral, the appropriate use of resources is hospitality. Guests are welcomed as members of the family in the home of their host. Guests are fed, protected and honored for the duration of their stay.

I am not suggesting that Western economics are bad and first-century Jewish economics were ideal. Both have their problems and limitations. But the perspective of resources as limited or unlimited greatly impacts how we view power and its stewardship. If we view power as limitless, then we don't think too much about its stewardship. We have a consumer attitude toward power: We can use it when we need it. It belongs to us individually. We can cultivate it and manage it and distribute it for the outcomes we believe are necessary. However, the problem with this perspective is that a social setting does not afford limitless amounts of power to everyone present. In a bounded social space, if one person takes up lots of room with his or her presence, others cannot have the same measure of influence. Power as a resource has limits. The stewardship of power, then, is not consumption but hospitality toward the rest of the "family." The purpose of having power is not to enhance or secure one's personal influence but to enhance the influence and well-being of the group. If power is used to create a healthy, harmonious space, the group has more emotional and mental resources to fulfill the call of Christ.

Jesus used his power to invite others into his personal space. Acknowledging the hemorrhaging woman who touched him, touching the leper, calling to Bartimaeus the blind beggar—all are instances where Jesus invited the powerless, the outsider, the desperate into the sacred space around him. The individual was then given status and access to what Jesus had to offer. In a culture valuing honor, Jesus, the one with honor, cleansed those with shame by bringing them into his personal—and intimate, we could argue—space. The observers in the social setting would accept the honor bestowed upon that person, unless they had already rejected Jesus, as many of the religious leaders had. Physical proximity to Jesus had the power to heal these individuals and restore them to the community in a redeemed role. Jesus used his status to empower others and to subvert the status quo. His gestures of inclusion demonstrate how power can be manifested through discreet actions in social space. Jesus stewarded his words, his use of touch, the orientation of his body—in short, his presence—to love those marginalized by the culture.

In Christian culture, religious leaders—pastors, lay leaders, parachurch leaders and academics—have power in social space and public space. The temptation is to use that power to maintain current religious and social systems that assure their status and authority. Words, gestures, and body orientation become tools for exclusion—to demarcate between who does and does not belong. Power is acquired, managed and distributed to make sure that the present system and power brokers are preserved rather than transformed. At a conference in Eagle, Idaho, Brian McLaren told a story about a group of pastors who refused to maintain the status quo.[11] They were pastors of a large church in a denomination that didn't ordain women, and they were struggling with how to acknowledge the gifts of a woman who served with them. They wanted to recognize her anointed preaching and teaching gifts, but didn't see how they could do it. After studying Scripture, praying and fasting for quite some time, they felt led by God to ordain this woman. When the denominational leaders found out, they told the pastors they couldn't ordain a woman. The pastors responded that they already had. Then the denominational leaders threatened them with various consequences if they didn't revoke the ordination. In the end, the male pastors gave up their ordination, saying, "We will all be called teachers." They acted not as consumers trying to preserve their status but as hosts using their power to include one whom they believed God wanted them to include.

THEREFORE . . .

How we use power in social spaces communicates our motivations, needs and passions. We spend hours in the church and at conferences discussing how to bring more people into relationship with Jesus Christ, how to transform lives and communities, without acknowledging one of the most fundamental forces in our nature: power.

Understanding power as a group resource rather than an individual one could unleash a new freedom among us, a freedom that entails stewarding power as a group resource for accomplishing God's purposes. The value in having large amounts of social power is the ability to bring the powerless into a grace-filled space where both the powerful and powerless experience transformation. Power is not shunned or hidden. Acquiring power is an important act of spiritual stewardship. In fact, a person cannot be a servant leader without the power and personal capacity to influence. It does not come through the divestment of power but through its use for redemptive purposes. It is an invitation to God's feast rather than to personal security and exclusion. Leighton Ford modeled this by using his presence and power to mentor young leaders spiritually and professionally.

The attitude that power in social space is unlimited rather than limited creates an isolating, consumerist spirit rather than a spirit of hospitality. When power is seen as unlimited, the conclusion is that a person's power or lack thereof is an individual responsibility and not for the group to address. But when we adopt the model of Jesus, those with large amounts of social power have a primary responsibility to steward it—to monitor it, assess it and use it well for the benefit of the whole group.

QUESTIONS FOR DISCUSSION

1. How has the consumerist economics of unlimited goods impacted Western culture? How have you seen it affect a leader's use of power?

2. How might the perspective of social power as a limited resource inform your actions on a committee or team?

3. How might hospitality as a response to consumerism affect leadership in your church or organization?

4. Assess how you steward your own power resources. How might you acquire, distribute and manage your power, both as an individual and on a team?

9

SPACE-TAKING AND SPACE-HIDING

Using Power Well

You shall not pass!
GANDALF IN *THE FELLOWSHIP OF THE RING*

You can't push a rope.
JOHN ROESER

Power in social space varies from person to person and from place to place. The amount of space we take up falls on a continuum from lots to little, depending on the setting. Power is used well when the extreme edges of the continuum are brought to the middle. Leaders who function on the "lots of space" end are like sponges soaking up influence and power. On the other end are leaders who are more like shadows, having little impact regardless of their passion to make a difference. Shadows think they are true servant leaders, but they are actually invisible when it comes to influencing change. Sponges also think they are true servant leaders, but they are often absorbed in their own agendas and needs, unaware of how their presence impacts the group. Shadows influence little, and sponges soak up the influence capacity in the room. Stewarding power well means both types of leaders bring their gifts to the center rather than living at the edges. Both the powerful and the powerless have things to learn about their leadership.

JAKE'S STORY: DRIVEN TO THE SHADOWS

Jake, an associate pastor of a megachurch in the South, shared this story of a frustrating meeting of the senior pastor, his staff and the chair of the deacons:

> I couldn't figure out what to say, and I didn't know how to enter the discussion. The senior pastor and the chair of the deacons were pushing for change in our leadership structure. I understood the need for some reform in how we were doing things, but it seemed like the issue had already been decided. The new structure didn't really address the underlying problem of people in the congregation feeling burned-out and not wanting to volunteer for more. Because they were being asked over and over to serve, people were starting to slip away to other churches.
>
> Before the meeting, I had e-mailed everyone a study called *Where Are the Volunteers?* which described our situation exactly. It also gave some principles and suggestions for change. But I don't think anyone even read it!!
>
> I've been the associate pastor for fifteen years, but in meetings, it's as if I'm not even there. I wonder why I'm even kept around. I feel like a toy soldier sitting on the shelf. I'm there but never in the thick of things. I think the senior pastor keeps me around because I get lots of work done and I don't make waves. I didn't sign up for this type of calling. I want to make a difference for Christ in the lives of his people, not use them up in programming.

Jake was a leader without power. He knew why people were slipping out the back doors of the church, but no one listened to him, even when he supported his insights with a study. Jake had a deep passion for the mission of the church, but his voice was ignored. He was a shadow, not by choice but by circumstance. Jake felt it was his job to support the senior pastor, but he was troubled by this leader's growing inability to hear any voice other than his own. Jake wanted to be a servant leader, not a troublemaker. Yet he had spent fifteen years working as a servant with little influence as a leader, and he had reached his limit. He wanted to take ownership of his calling and gifts to lead.

Servant leadership is not about blind service to other authority figures. It is about gifts, calling, skills and passion laid down at the feet of Jesus. Being a servant leader means being obedient to what Jesus called us to do and to be. Simply getting things done for Jesus is not the same as leading like Jesus. But we can all fall into the trap of serving a leader who poorly manages his or her power. Such a leader takes up more and more space in a limited-goods environment, so others are driven more and more to the shadows. Jake was right; the senior pastor needed him to be a toy soldier, not a real one. Jake could stay in the shadows or move on.

CARL'S STORY: GROUP SHADOW-THINK

Carl, a new pastor at a Friends church, told me about an encounter he had with an eighty-five-year-old member, a gentleman who always needed to participate in open worship. In a Friends church, open worship is a period of silence for listening to the Holy Spirit, who might provide guidance or teaching to an individual or to the congregation. If the message is for the congregation, the person who receives it stands up and shares. If the words are to an individual, the person keeps quiet. Usually there is more silence than talking during open worship. However, this elderly Friend talked every single Sunday, sometimes for twenty minutes. His words were difficult to follow and rarely added to the congregation's worship. New and longtime members alike complained to Carl about the man's ramblings. When Carl spoke to him about it, he said, "Pastor, you need to talk to the Lord about this. It sounds like a personal problem. I only say what the Lord wants me to say, and if you don't like it, then you just don't like anyone getting in the way of what you want to do, and that's sad." He added, "I've been coming to this church for fifty-five years. How long have you been here?" Carl was at his wits' end. The longtime member was monopolizing the social space, and the result was not good. Not only did he take up space, he believed he was righteous in doing so. And for more than fifty-five years, the elders had said nothing to him. It was left to Carl, the newcomer, to try to take care of it.

It's a common problem. One person dominates the scene, and no one in the group does much about it, even after years of misery. The group rationalizes that it's just the way the person is, so they grin and bear it. In reality, though, the gentleman in Carl's story got that way because the congregation allowed it. He took up space during open worship because the others gave it to him, over and over again. The group collectively and instinctively chose not to muddy the waters by confronting him. Being a sponge is not simply a personal choice; it is enabled by the group.

Sponges are sponges because the group either needs them to be or simply lets them be. Shadows are shadows for the same reasons. Why else would this Quaker church allow one individual to soak up "spiritual glory" every week when it was neither liked nor appreciated? Why, over the course of fifty-five years, had no one said something to this man? What were they afraid to lose? The church settled for one self-absorbed man instead of the chance for a weekly experience of Christ's presence in worship. Why? Many people believe taking up space is an individual act rather than a group decision, so they live with the consequences. Over the years this man began to abuse his role as a spiritual voice in the church, perhaps because of his lineage or his pocketbook. The congregation got used to it, or they didn't want to make waves or hurt anyone. Groups often don't want to face the messy consequences of addressing a problem, even if the problem has a toxic impact on the group.

During a meeting, space-takers generally speak first or last, when everyone else is done, or they speak extensively. Often they are insecure leaders, and they try to mask it by controlling the social environment. Space-hiders often talk outside of a meeting about the things they wanted to say but didn't. Both types are absorbed in their individual realities and fail to consider the reality of the whole. The collective, unspoken response to these behaviors is groupthink. For situations involving the misuse of social space, I call it "shadow-think." When a group wants to minimize conflict or stay in a comfort zone, it avoids challenging an individual's misuse of power.

Shadow-think happens when individual doubts, ideas or intuitions are put aside for fear of upsetting group harmony. Group members might think it is better to be peaceful than ethical. So the person taking up space is not challenged. However, if the purpose of the group is to be light to the world, then allowing one person to soak up all the space is a misuse of power. The only way forward is to come to the center—the group in the shadows has to come out and dry up the sponge. In Carl's situation, shadow-think was long entrenched in the group. The elderly Friend was on one end of the continuum and the congregation on the other. Carl could lead the effort to bring everyone toward the center, but only with the full conviction of the elders that the elderly member's behavior was un-Friendly.

THE STORY OF A PASTOR'S WIFE: MAKING GOD THE GREAT SPONGE

A female leader shared this story with me:

> In this particular church, the strong and powerful made the rules. The "regular" people basically did what they were told. One year the women's group was holding their annual election for new officers. The nominating committee spoke with one woman in particular about placing her name on the ballot for president, and she said yes. The names of the nominees for all the offices were printed and distributed. However, when it came time to vote, the pastor's wife announced that God had revealed to her who should be the president of the women's group. She emphasized that this was not her choice but God's. If the group didn't vote accordingly, they would not be going against her but against God. The next thing you know, the nominations were thrown out and the pastor's wife had selected the leader.

One of the oldest power ploys in history is equating one's personal agenda with God's. Who can argue with that? Often no one does. When we hear the words "God told me" or some variation, we find it difficult to challenge the person speaking them. Even though God's character and purposes are clearly described in Scripture, and it is unlikely that Jesus would act in such a manner, we still get confused and back off. God then becomes the great sponge, with the spokesperson being the obedient servant. The reality is just the opposite. Unhealthy leaders play the "God card" to enhance their own position and their own agenda. They take on the role of the sponge and put God in service to their whims. A group accepts the God card because they don't want to take responsibility for the consequences of bucking a leader or because the shadows are abdicating their influence for the safety of being unseen. Either way, God is rarely part of the equation.

In a top-down organizational structure, it is difficult to challenge someone at the top who uses God as the great sponge. However, the group's true responsibility is to keep Christ—not their leader—at the center. Those closest to the puffed-up leader have a responsibility to bring him or her out from behind the "God curtain," just as Dorothy and her companions did in the *Wizard of Oz*. The real wizard was hiding behind a curtain, using special effects to portray himself as a fierce, powerful creature when actually he was quite a small and ordinary man. Pulling a leader from behind the God curtain is not easy and involves enormous risk, but in the long run it is worth it. A leader with a personal agenda does not get the same spiritual results as a leader who guides a group through a discernment process with the Holy Spirit. The latter takes more time, self-awareness, patience and prayerfulness, but the outcome is more in sync with God's character and purpose. In a healthy setting, regardless of the leadership structure, the person with power makes an effort to bring everyone to the center for an honest and prayerful discernment process.

THE DILEMMA OF COMING TO THE CENTER

We identify with these stories. They lead us to ask questions such as, how do leaders driven to the shadows move to the center so their voice is heard? How does an individual accomplish that without sabotaging his or her future in the group? On the other hand, how do leaders who take up lots of space stop absorbing power and begin to steward it in healthy ways? The dilemma for the shadows is that they want to make a difference but don't know how. The dilemma for the sponges is that they are often unaware of their negative impact on the group's decision-making processes. How do they both come to the center?

There are many complicated psychological, social and cultural reasons why some people have more space and others less, as noted in previous chapters. For example, if you continually feel ignored or invisible to others, you begin to question your own value. If you question your value, you're less likely to upset the status quo. Carol Gilligan, writing about self-confidence changes in her daughter noted, "Because girls, by adolescence, are mature enough to recognize and reflect on what's happening to them, they reveal a process of initiation that exacts a psychological cost. Seventeen-year-old Iris, the valedictorian of her class, observes, 'If I were to say what I was thinking and feeling, no one would want to be with me; *my voice would be too loud.*'"[1] The socialization process of adolescent girls can compel them to moderate their behavior to a more submissive stance. Iris's adaptation to her environment involved the forces of her peers, her culture and her life experience.

The same is true for leaders. They adapt to their environment because of social forces, culture and their own life experiences. These variables, and more, converge to maintain the status quo. Bucking an entrenched system is difficult but may be necessary. However, before we move on to strategies, we need to consider how the experience of power triggers darker forces in our own lives. It's easy to behave when you're powerless—not so much when you have power.

POWER PROJECTION AND POWER STRUGGLES

Whenever two or more individuals gather for a common purpose, whether a family, a business team or a small group going deeper in Christ, power dynamics are triggered. Power is exercised any time a person in a group attempts to influence, perhaps through an opinion, suggestion, passionate plea, rational presentation or the use of his or her body to take up space. The attempt to influence is received, ignored or shelved for the time being. If received, others have incorporated the idea or emotion into their own psyche, deciding how it fits. If ignored, the idea or emotion didn't get through the front door of the mind, or it entered only to be considered and then rejected. Usually groups make final decisions after hearing from the traditional influencer in the group.

Power is not perceived through simple rational analysis. The dynamics of power between people in a group trigger an inner psychological struggle between feelings of security and value, which can be strengthened or hurt by the person who has power. Therefore, whoever is perceived as having the most power, whoever is taking up the most space, will either attract or threaten persons who have less ego definition or less status in the group. For this reason, people who possess many natural space-taking assets attract a coalition of "yes-people," and shadow-think becomes an easy pitfall. Insecure people or leaders who are on the way up the ladder will attach themselves to the powerful. They project onto the leader their own desires for success and value.

Power projection often results in a codependent relationship between the leader and the followers. The leader likes and enjoys the support and devotion of an inner circle. The followers have the status that goes along with access to insider power. The outcome is an unhealthy leadership environment in which the needs and egos of the leader and his or her followers supersede the needs of their community. A healthy leadership environment is possible when the leader does not allow this to happen. Then group members have the opportunity to take responsibility for their own needs. In a healthy power environment, the leader and group members feel comfortable raising contrary opinions. Vigorous debates about issues do not become personal attacks on an opponent's character or motives. Power isn't soaked up by a select few but is shared in the group. The leader and group members serve a larger vision and purpose that goes beyond their own needs for status and security.

Another response is the power struggle. Instead of the group members projecting onto the leader their needs for value and success, they react against the leader. The motivation for power struggles is the same as projection: insecurity about value, identity or status in a group. Power struggles are expressed through open rebellion, passive-aggressive behavior or attacks (direct or indirect) on the character or decisions of the leader. People who are reactive might display anger, make accusations, cry tears of frustration or garner support from others in the system. A leader sometimes finds that a few people will always attack or rebel no matter how safe a leader he or she might be. A healthy leader is not enough; the group may or may not be able to handle power in healthy ways. Jesus was often attacked. Other religious leaders perceived him as a threat. People followed him or hated him for reasons that had nothing to do with his message of love. The same happens to leaders today.

Power struggles are ego struggles. The group's situation is unhealthy if the leader does not create safe space in the center for all voices to contribute and for all members to thoughtfully consider the input of others. If you are the leader and you feel threatened by someone who disagrees with you, has different ideas or makes a point that is quite brilliant but one you didn't come up with first, then you have ego issues. You have spiritual and emotional work to do. Some members of the group might be unhealthy, contributing to your frustration, but until you as the leader can understand and manage your own reactivity, you won't be able to influence the group toward health.

If you are a healthy leader but one or two members of the group get into power struggles with you, you have options. The first is to try to mentor and coach the individuals into greater self-awareness. Sir Ernest Shackleton, the British Antarctic explorer, saved the lives of his entire crew under impossible circumstances after they were shipwrecked and stranded for two years. One of the reasons for his remarkable success was that he kept those who complained the most in his own tent. He cultivated a relationship with them and isolated them from damaging the morale of the others.[2] But we're not stranded on an ice floe. If, after months of honest connection and mentoring, you still find that someone is unwilling to reflect on his or her own role in the power struggle, move that person off your team. If that is not possible, prayer and discernment can lead you to another creative option. Ignoring the power struggle is never an option.

If you are not the primary leader of a group but your leadership space is continually invaded by the leader, it is not a safe situation. If you draw boundaries and ask the leader to respect them, yet he or she does not, it is not a safe place. If your ideas are confiscated, if you're ignored, if you feel used, then the sponge is not staying out of your space. If you are in a direct reporting relationship to this person, you might start praying about finding another job. Life is too precious, good teams are too much fun, and money does not buy happiness, so don't exchange your financial security for your emotional wholeness.

In reality, it is rarely *just* the group members or *just* the leader who is unhealthy. It's a mess of both. That is why the group—not just one or two persons in power—must reflect on their power resources and the use and management of that power. In a healthy group, each person is constantly monitoring his or her use of power during group processes. Everyone moves naturally and easily across the continuum from taking space to sharing space to being still and back again. Each one discerns when and when not to take up space. Sometimes it's best to be still and listen because you have nothing to add. At other times it's best to speak up because you have something valuable to offer. Sometimes you're in the middle, with everyone actively considering an idea on the table. Each person in the group feels this freedom to take up space, to be still or to be active while working together. The goal is that no one is labeled a sponge or a shadow. Instead, there is freedom for everyone to move in and out of the center.

SPACE-SERVING: JESUS' USE OF POWER

Jesus never acted small. He wasn't a shadow who stayed in the background. On the other hand, Jesus never acted big, like a sponge soaking up lots of social space. Instead, he embedded his presence and power in his followers so they might thrive. Jesus said to his disciples, "I will not leave you orphaned; I am coming to you. In a little while the world will no longer see me, but you will see me; because I live, you also will live. On that day you will know that I am in my Father, and you in me, and I in you" (Jn 14:18-20). Paul wrote of "Christ in you, the hope of glory" (Col 1:27). Jesus' use of power was guided by his perfect love and justice. That same capacity is in believers, so their presence in the world has the same influencing potential. Jesus is our model for the space-serving use of power.

In Luke 13:10-17 Jesus heals a woman who had been crippled for eighteen years. He healed her in public on the sabbath in the synagogue. The sabbath was commanded by God as a day of rest, yet Jesus often chose to heal people on that day. His healing activities on the sabbath angered the religious leaders, whose role it was to teach and model holiness. A primary means of modeling holiness was strictly adhering to the Jewish laws, which included doing no work—not even healing—on the sabbath. Jesus, on the other hand, often broke these religious laws. He modeled holiness not through compliance with religious laws but through love and compassion, even if an act of love broke one of those laws, as in this story from Luke.

The opening verses alert the reader to the struggles about to unfold: "Now he was teaching in one of the synagogues on the sabbath. And just then there appeared a woman with a spirit that had crippled her for eighteen years. She was bent over and was quite unable to stand up straight." Jesus, in the role of a rabbi teaching on the sabbath, would have been reading a text from the Scriptures and then expound on its meaning. Women were allowed to be in a synagogue, but they would have been in a separate section in the back or in an upper balcony screened off from view. The scene would have included synagogue officials and other men near Jesus at the front. Into the story enters a human being with a litany of characteristics labeling her marginalized status in the social system. She was without honor and without place, completely in the shadows. Luke's use of the Greek word *idou,* meaning "behold" and translated here as "just then," highlights the unexpectedness and shock of this woman's appearance in the synagogue.

The first strike against this individual was her gender. In that culture, men and women did not mix in public. A woman's status was secondary to that of men. Second, she had a "spirit" of sickness. A condition like hers was not attributed solely to physical problems but to spiritual and social ones. If a person was ill, sin was seen as part of the equation and resulted in the loss of social standing and reputation in the community. Third, the eighteen-year duration of her illness indicated that no confession, sacrifice, healers or medicines had helped her. And fourth, she was completely unable to stand upright. She was always looking down, at her own shame. This woman had no social power. She was a mere shadow, hardly considered valuable to her community. The social chasm between a rabbi teaching in a synagogue and a woman bent over for eighteen years can hardly be fathomed in contemporary Western thought. Because we would see her condition as a medical problem, her physical condition would not impact her intrinsic value in our contemporary social setting, as it would in the story.

We read: "When Jesus saw her, he called her over and said, 'Woman, you are set free from your ailment.' When he laid his hands on her, immediately she stood up straight and began praising God." Jesus did more than just notice the woman and then continue his teaching to the attentive men. He didn't just make a mental note to talk with her at the end of the service or the next day. She'd been crippled for eighteen years, so what would a few more hours or another day matter? Teaching brilliantly in the synagogue on the sabbath and then arranging for a public healing the next day might have given Jesus prestige and legitimacy. However, instead of soaking up more status, Jesus began a series of maneuvers that could have been considered political suicide. First, he called the woman over to him. He brought an unclean woman into a group of men on the sabbath. By bringing her into his social space, Jesus was extending his space to her. Second, with his authority he healed her sickness. Third, he laid hands on her. He touched her, which, in the eyes of the officials, meant he contaminated himself with the spirit of her illness. Yet she was healed, and her first response was to glorify God. She stood up straight and praised God.

The response of the witnesses was immediate: "But the leader of the synagogue, indignant because Jesus had cured on the sabbath, kept saying to the crowd, 'There are six days on which work ought to be done; come on those days and be cured, and not on the sabbath day.'" The leader of the synagogue challenged Jesus' honor by naming the most obvious offense, breaking God's commandment not to work on the Sabbath. Only a peer of Jesus could have challenged his honor in public. A person of lesser status would not have dared, and a person of greater status wouldn't have bothered. The synagogue leader appealed to the crowd to make the conclusion that Jesus was a sinner and a fraud. A power struggle was in play. Honor, the most valued resource, was at stake. Honor was more important than anything else, even money. Poverty was a lack of social connections and status, not just personal wealth. Honor, like physical resources, was also limited. The Pharisees and Sadducees continually vied to diminish Jesus' power and enhance their own by acquiring more honor or confirming the honor they already had.

Jesus needed to respond to the synagogue leader's challenge. If he did not—if he acted embarrassed or made excuses or said nothing—

he would lose face with the crowd. While the synagogue leader kept stirring up the crowd with Jesus' great offense, Jesus challenged him with an insult.

> But the Lord answered him and said, "You hypocrites! Does not each of you on the sabbath untie his ox or his donkey from the manger, and lead it away to give it water? And ought not this woman, a daughter of Abraham whom Satan bound for eighteen long years, be set free from this bondage on the sabbath day?" When he said this, all his opponents were put to shame; and the entire crowd was rejoicing at all the wonderful things that he was doing.

Jesus called these leaders hypocrites, insulting them before the crowd. Jesus used the shamed woman's condition to publicly shame the leaders. He named their hypocrisy. They "worked" on the sabbath by untying their animals to give them water, and yet they were not willing to provide for the needs of a woman bent over like a beast of burden. The length of her suffering was all the more reason for compassion rather than judgment. Jesus calls her not a poor woman but "a daughter of Abraham," a descendant and heir of the Jewish people. Thus he restored her to her original social position in the community. Jesus' response to the woman's plight—healing her and restoring her despite challenges by those in authority—pleased the crowd. They rejoiced, and the leaders were shamed.

Jesus did not act like a shadow, playing it safe to protect himself or to avoid angering others. Neither did Jesus act like a sponge, using all the attention and social power he had to impose his kingship on others. He took the crippled woman from humiliation to honor as a beloved daughter of the King. Jesus' aim was to bring more people into the family of God. He modeled how taking up space in hostile environments can lead to redemption when others are brought into the center of his light. He also faced the risks involved, but he didn't fear suffering.

SO THEN . . .

Like Jesus, we are priests. That is our spiritual identity. Because we abide in Christ and follow him, we publicly live out his presence. Because we have his presence, influence happens naturally. Having too little influence (hiding in the shadows) or using influence for personal gain (soaking up space like a sponge) is uncharacteristic of a follower of Christ. The use of power to heal and to honor, like Jesus did, is both grand and humbling. It is grand in the power of redemption to shape eternity, and humbling in the simplicity of sharing space with someone else.

The friend of a pastor told him the story of standing on the corner of 2nd and Broadway across from the New York Stock Exchange during a ticker tape parade for soldiers returning from Desert Storm. It was a huge event. Colin Powell and other dignitaries were there to honor these soldiers. Everyone was going crazy over these men and women. Standing near the friend was a Vietnam veteran dressed in his uniform. One of the Desert Storm soldiers saw him, got out of formation and walked up to the vet. He saluted the older man, then hugged and thanked him. The Desert Storm soldier shared his moment of glory with someone who hadn't gotten such a moment. He brought the Vietnam vet into his space and honored him for his sacrifice.

A Presbyterian pastor once said in a sermon, "If you seek power before service, you'll neither get power, nor serve. If you seek to serve people more than to gain power, you will not only serve people, you will gain influence. That's very much the way Jesus did it."[3] Our challenge is to be part of God's kingdom and get in the game as Jesus did. God did not design us to be benchwarmers; we are all players. And since we are all part of this great game, with one great mission—to be Christ's light to a dark world—everyone gets to play. Everyone *needs* to play, whether we are more comfortable as shadows or sponges. Shadows need get out of the corners and off the benches and engage in the activity of life happening all around them. Sponges need to take positions as coaches to model and guide the execution of the game. Both need to come to the center. The goal is for everyone to take responsibility for God's purposes by serving when called to serve, which means leading when called to lead. Not everyone will have a designated leadership role, but everyone will be a part of leadership in their home, community or place of work or ministry.

QUESTIONS FOR DISCUSSION

1. Would you describe yourself as a space-taker or space-hider? Share an example of a situation that led you to this insight.

2. Would your peers or your work or ministry group agree with your assessment of yourself in social space?

3. Have you ever been attacked as a leader because of your role, gender or personality? If so, how did you handle it?

4. Assuming you are a healthy leader who handles your role well, what would you do if a member of your group persistently attacked or criticized your efforts?

5. Read Mark 2:1-12. Using what you've learned so far, examine the power dynamics in the story of the paralytic and his four friends.

10

OPEN SPACE

Managing Our Own Souls

If it is a matter of power,
behold, He is the strong one!
JOB 19:19 NASB

> Over the years, I have become a
> strong believer in the fact that the
> external world can be changed by
> altering our internal world.
> ROBERT QUINN

Jesus' capacity to continually absorb insults and engage in honor disputes came from a deep place of inner preparedness and quiet. In the story of Simon and the sinner woman, analyzed in chapter three, Jesus ignored Simon's insults. He wasn't even fazed by the Pharisee's lack of hospitality. Jesus still took a position at the table as a guest, and he addressed Simon as a teacher would, with the traditional words, "I have something to say to you." Jesus took up space by telling a story rather than overtly pointing out Simon's mistakes. He did not allow the leadership moment to pass, despite the hostile environment. Jesus didn't overreact, go off in a huff or whine to his disciples about the poor treatment. Because of Jesus' words and actions, possibly Simon developed more compassion toward others, but for sure a lost woman's honor and future was restored. The same thing happened in the story of the crippled woman. Jesus took the opportunity to teach and model the true nature of God's kingdom by healing the woman despite the hostile environment.

It is not possible to step into public experiences like Jesus did without first spending considerable time managing our own souls, emotions and minds. Paul exhorted Timothy, his protégé, to "be prepared in season and out of season" (2 Tim 4:2 NIV). The command translated "be prepared" is a Greek military term meaning "to stay at one's post," to be on duty no matter what. The phrase "in season and out of season" suggests that we need to be prepared whether it is convenient or not. As representatives of Christ's kingdom, we are always on deck. Our presence and potential for influencing is part of daily life. There isn't a "now I'm a leader" or "now I might influence" time. We are always living our lives as an offering of Christ's hospitality—anywhere, anytime. Therefore, it is imperative that we eat regularly from Christ's table. We need to spend time in our spiritual closets to clear our heads of the constant buzz of life. We should not lead or attempt to influence without preparing ourselves.

One of David Goleman's premises in *Emotional Intelligence* is that self-leadership is the distinguishing factor between good leaders and great leaders.[1] Self-leadership means leading and managing yourself first. Management expert Dee Hock found that one of the consistent distinguishing factors between great leaders and ordinary leaders is that great leaders spend 40 percent of their time in what he calls "self-leadership" functions: "If you look to lead, invest at least 40% of your time managing yourself—your ethics, character, prin-

ciples, purpose, motivation, and conduct."[2] Time spent alone reading, thinking, preparing, and for us Christians, praying actively and
reflectively, is necessary to lead as Jesus led.

Some situations require even more prayer and reflection. Before
Jesus began his ministry, he spent forty days in the desert. Before
he chose his twelve disciples, he went to a mountain to pray all
night. Before he went to the cross, he spent hours praying in the
garden of Gethsemane. Crucial transitions, meetings or conversations that have huge consequences for a person or group require
thoughtful preparation. Some leaders think that the up-front investment in preparation is not always necessary because experience and
intuition can get you through. If crucial times were purely rational,
that might be true. However, high-stakes events trigger intense emotions, which can lead to clouded judgment. Leaders might then become reactive in an effort to protect their turf.

Protecting your own turf is referred to by social scientists as *terri-
toriality*. Violation of a person's space is often experienced as a violation of self-identity. Territorial responses are physical, psychological
or both. Children are physical when they protect their turf, whether
it is the right to sit in grandpa's lap or the ownership of a certain toy.
Adults also instinctively stake out territory that defines their place
in a group, but hopefully they do it without pushing and shoving.
Instead, adults might use other physical markers, such as setting
down a coffee mug in front of a chair at a meeting table, then going
off to do something else. Someone else sets down a pencil and paper
or drapes a sweater or jacket over the back of a chair to mark his or
her territory. We don't need an experienced guide to tell us what
these physical markers mean.

In the same way, we have verbal markers that are readily interpreted by those familiar with the culture. Introductions are exam-
ples of verbal turf markers:

- "This is my wife."
- "This is my best friend."
- "This is Dr. Olvera from the United Nations serving on the International Court of Justice."
- "This is my pastor."
- "This is the Right Reverend Doctor Hildegard Jefferson."

Each introduction identifies the territory of the one being introduced and the one making the introduction. A lack of understanding can lead to a turf struggle. Adults rarely use force to protect their turf, but they will use psychological actions, such as being passive-aggressive. For instance, they might exclude someone from receiving insider information, or from a conversation or event. Another common way of excluding others is using language, jokes or references to history that only insiders would know.

Protecting turf, whether it's sitting at a particular place in a meeting or fulfilling a particular role in a group, is instinctive. If one individual is the resident expert on an issue, but the group looks to a newcomer for expertise instead, that person might get territorial. If a person is criticized for an event for which he or she had responsibility, that person might get angry. When turf is challenged, emotions are evoked. When emotions are evoked, behaviors become less rational and more defensive and reactive. Therefore, any time an important meeting or conversation is planned, it is essential that leaders prepare spiritually and emotionally for *their own* reaction.

EVAN'S STORY

Evan, the pastor of a church plant in Tennessee, went to a local retreat center for an entire day of praying and seeking God's guidance for the next strategic steps for his church. The church was a year old and doing well, but it seemed to Evan that something was lacking. The worship was great. There was energy and enthusiasm for the mission, but something was missing. Evan believed people weren't going deeper in faith. They were enjoying being part of the church, but their lives weren't being transformed, and Evan wanted to resolve that. After spending the day in prayer, he felt God leading him to start small groups for accountability, spiritual formation and prayer. He was excited about his vision and his motto, "Small Groups Work." He thought this would be a practical, less-intimidating approach to going deeper in faith.

At the next elders' meeting, Evan enthusiastically presented his vision and plans for a four-week series of messages on the topic, which he would start in two weeks. Immediately the elders started asking probing questions: Do we have trained leaders? What kind of groups will we start? Will all the groups do the same thing, or will the leader of each group decide on its focus? How will you make sure that everyone who wants to be in a group gets into one? How will you make sure that those who step forward to lead are healthy individuals on track with the church's mission? On and on the questions went. The elders weren't convinced about the whole idea. Evan felt defensive and angry. They just didn't get it; they were sabotaging his plans—God's plans. He stood up and started pacing. He began to quote Scripture, use theological language about koinonia and covenant, and talk about people in church history who brought renewal through small groups. Soon the elders weren't saying much, and the chair adjourned the meeting.

Later Evan realized he had blown it. The next morning he spent extra time in prayer and reflection. All he wanted was to lead—not to deal with these secondary issues that were just making his job harder. After an hour of sitting quietly with Christ, Evan understood that his own strong emotions came from the growing fatigue that often plagues church planters. He was so busy. He was trying to get things done and keep the momentum going, but as a result he had gotten sloppy. The meeting the night before was a wake-up call. The elders had asked good questions. They had a right to make sure that whatever was brought before the church community was carefully thought out and would result in real growth, not just the addition of another program. He called each elder to apologize and thank them for their input, and he asked for volunteers to serve with him on a team to think through all the issues.

From then on, whenever Evan brought a major issue to the elders, he set aside extra time during his morning devotions to examine his own motivations and emotions. He prayed he would be filled with Christ, not his fears. He asked himself two questions: (1) What strong feelings might be triggered in me? (2) Have I carefully thought through all the implications of this proposal and the processes needed to implement it? As he prayed, he went beyond seeking out the next step or solution to a problem and examined his own heart to make sure it would be unconflicted in the face of potential challenges.

INNER PREPAREDNESS

Whether you are the leader or a member of a committee or team, coming together to carry out the business of a church or Christian organization is sacred work. It is ministry. It is the epicenter, the heart, of that place. Therefore, emotional, mental and spiritual preparation is critical. Being in a position of influence, no matter how humble, requires attentiveness to one's inner life. As the light of Christ, our primary responsibility is to connect to him and allow the Holy Spirit access to our hearts and souls. The following are practical suggestions for developing this inner preparedness.

Open space for spiritual attentiveness. The primary ingredients for spiritual attentiveness are time and space. Enough time is needed to experience rest and openness with God. A quiet and reflective space is necessary to minimize distractions and allow

the inner emotional psyche and spirit to surface. The Holy Spirit
moves in us at those deeper levels. When we fill up inner space
with our own words and thoughts, we are trying to stay in control. When we allow ourselves to be still and wait, we relinquish
control to God. Open space with God is not simply leisure or
selfishness; it is our spiritual food and drink. In Tony Hendra's
book *Father Joe: The Man Who Saved My Soul,* the priest says this
about listening to God:

> The only way to know God, the only way to know the other,
> is to listen. Listening is reaching out into that unknown other
> self, surmounting your walls and theirs: listening is the begin-
> ning of understanding, the exercise of love. . . . We must listen
> because we are so often wrong in our certainties. When we
> pass a motion in the chaotic debating chamber of our heads,
> it's never completely right, or even, most of the time, half right.
> The only way to edge closer to the truth is to listen with com-
> plete openness, bringing to the process no preconceptions,
> nothing prepared.[3]

Open space varies from person to person. Some find it outdoors
walking, gardening or running, where the rhythm of the physical
activity allows the inner life to surface. Others find it while using
their hands to create art or crafts. Most of us just need a quiet space
to sit. It is best to return to the same spot with the same rituals. I'm a
morning person, so that's where I find my open space. I prepare tea
in my china teapot. I get my journal, Bible and the Book of Common
Prayer. I go outside, weather permitting, and sit on the back patio.
In no particular order, I write in my journal, read my Bible, pray and
have stretches of silence. Almost without fail, my most creative moments or insights into difficult situations or understandings about
myself and others rise out of the open space and the silence. I don't
plan for it. I don't think about it. I'm just being present with God.

During those times, the Holy Spirit unravels the tight knots that busy lives often become tangled in.

If you find it difficult to experience open space without getting anxious about your busy day, use a timer. Remove all other time-keeping devices, and let the timer watch time for you. Have a note-pad and pen close by to write down random thoughts about things you need to do. Our bodies are conditioned for stimulation, so it may take time to get your body comfortable with stillness. When you have open space in your day to be still with God, you will find that you can also create internal openness in busy places. This happens, for example, when you're in a meeting room, and like Christ you are able to be thoughtful and unhurried about using your power.

Open space for emotional attentiveness. Open space with God is also a good way to reflect on strong emotions that are triggered or might be triggered in interactions with others. Strong emotions are doorways to understanding yourself and your relationship to God.[4] In particular, pay attention to emotions such as anger, anxiety or fear, jealousy or frustration. The emotional triggers in a meeting or other social interaction are far more potent than the rational ones, yet we usually pay little attention to them. However, reflecting on emotional triggers develops self-awareness, which leads to a more clear-headed and redemptive experience the next time a power struggle or turf battle occurs.

In this process it is helpful to ask yourself "why" questions. If you are afraid, angry or anxious, or you might become so, ask yourself before Christ, *Why? Why am I feeling this way?* An answer will come. Continue asking yourself "why" until you get to the root cause of the emotion.[5] Almost always the core issue is a spiritual one.

Wayne, the pastor of a community church in Iowa, used this process to bring out some personal insights about a difficult inter-action he would soon have to face. Wayne had to tell the women's ministry leader, Andrea, that she was being let go. Because of her imperial leadership style, Andrea had problem after problem with volunteers. Even though Wayne had coached her and given her several opportunities to learn from her mistakes, Andrea insisted that she wasn't the problem. She blamed the volunteers, saying they didn't like her.

Wayne was anxious about the meeting with Andrea. He had arranged for another staff member to be present, but still he knew it wasn't going to be pretty. He set aside the morning to pray and collect himself. He had done this type of thing before, and it's always tough, but this time he was overly anxious. Before God, Wayne began to ask himself some "why" questions and think about his answers.

"Why am I dreading this meeting with Andrea?"

Well, I don't want to be hurt.

"Why don't I want to be hurt?"

Because I'm tired of being beat up by unhealthy people.

"Why does that bother me?"

Because most of my time is spent with individuals who have no intention of changing, and I end up as the pooper scooper of the church. I've got the scars to prove it.

"Why does it hurt me? Jesus got hit pretty hard by people who wouldn't change."

I don't know. I just wanted it to be wonderful, but I'm tired.

"Why am I tired?"

I'm tired . . . I'm tired because I've made this about me, my effort and my hurt. My energy comes from you, Lord. I do this for you. It's not about me. Forgive me for making this personal and not missional. Help me to see Andrea as you see her. Guide me to be clear and kind, but not shirk the hard stuff. You didn't. You are my Shepherd. I follow you to green pastures, not the Andreas to dark valleys.

The meeting with Andrea was hard, but Wayne felt calm. He followed the Holy Spirit's guidance during the conversation. He was able to put his anxiousness aside and focus on Andrea and the Holy Spirit's guidance. Despite the difficult situation, it went well.

Open space for rational attentiveness. Open space also allows us to thoughtfully engage the rational parts of ourselves. Our best thinking is necessary to respond to the complex tasks and ideas facing today's spiritual leaders. We need space to consider and study views contrary to our own. Truly understanding other perspectives helps us appreciate what matters to people. It's not possible to enter that type of critical reflection without space to do so. Often we spend most of our time supporting and selling our perspective rather than listening to all the options or trying to understand them better. A leader who uses his or her power well seeks to understand other views.

Taking time to think through and prepare ideas carefully leads to clarity. Leaders sometimes have an instinctive understanding of what needs to be done, but they fail to take the time to develop their thoughts. Instead, leaders (myself included) tend to say the same thing over and over again in a meeting trying to make an important point. Or they get emotionally intense. When a leader gets to that place, it's clear that the idea is more fuzzy instincts than clear direction. Instincts are necessary for good leadership, especially if we stay tuned in to the Holy Spirit. However, instincts also benefit from having time to take on clear form. Reading, studying, reflecting critically and forming clear ideas is part of inner preparedness for influence.

Brad, a member of the worship team of a suburban church in Kansas, felt the church needed to be regularly involved in local community service. He wanted the church to do more than serving Thanksgiving dinner at the homeless shelter or taking packages to the fire station for low-income kids at Christmas. Brad's first impulse was to stand up in the church's monthly business meeting and challenge the congregation to care about the poor like Jesus did. However, he decided to spend time praying about it and thinking it through. He did some research and discovered various community service options that matched the capacity and resources of the church. Brad considered the impact on other programs and how it would fit with the church's mission. He developed a tempered and compelling rationale for bringing this challenge to the church. When he brought the idea to the elders' board, he was ready for their questions. The board approved the proposal and made Brad chair of a team commissioned to bring this change to the church.

GETTING READY TO GET IN

When Jesus sent out the twelve disciples, he said to them, "See, I am sending you out like sheep into the midst of wolves; so be wise as serpents and innocent as doves" (Mt 10:16). A serpent symbolized cunning and cleverness; a dove symbolized purity. Having both a pure heart and a sharp mind is a difficult tension to maintain. To be clever, we must see the gray areas and pitfalls of a situation. To be pure, our motivation must come from Christ, not from personal fears or competitive pride. Jesus understood the leadership tension between critical thinking and a pure and undivided heart. We are the sheep and Jesus is our shepherd, but sometimes we serve among wolves. Without open space, I don't believe it's possible to keep our hearts connected to Christ and our minds sharp and vigilant. Our spiritual, emotional and rational processes are sifted in that open space, and the Holy Spirit motivates and guides us. Then it's more likely that we'll be ready to use our power well in the sandbox.

QUESTIONS FOR DISCUSSION

1. How do you create open space with God?

2. Is being quiet and nonproductive difficult for you? If so, why?

3. Share a recent leadership experience in which you had a strong emotional reaction. Using the "why" exercise, what are some insights you can gain from the experience?

4. Share a time when you researched and thought through an issue before presenting it to a group or leader, and describe the outcome.

5. Share a time when careful preparation of your spirit, emotions and thoughts made a difference in the outcome of a meeting or conversation.

11

GETTING IN THE SANDBOX

Practical Strategies

If you don't make a choice,
the choice makes you.
JOHNNY BLAZE
IN *GHOST RIDER*

Soon we must all face the choice
between what is right and what is easy.
DUMBLEDORE TO HARRY IN
HARRY POTTER AND THE GOBLET OF FIRE

Power is constructed in social settings, and your presence impacts how others perceive your leadership potential. You have a choice whether to engage in the leadership process or simply watch it. You can play in the sandbox or stay on the outside. If you want to influence as Christ did, you need practical strategies to help you get in the game.

MICHAEL'S STORY

Michael was a fullback-sized guy, an imposing figure of a man with a personality that was warm and laid-back. He had natural leadership potential. But he struggled with the impact he made in groups because he was so big and capable. He sensed that people treated him differently from others, and that confused him. It bothered him that people always turned to him for his opinion. He wanted to be a servant leader like Jesus, so he hung back. Even though he was the pastor of a growing, creative, emergent congregation in Ohio, he was hesitant to take up much leadership space. He encouraged others to lead, and he followed them even when he felt they were going in the wrong direction. Sometimes he complied with the group's will simply as a gesture of support and service. After hearing a presentation on the value of presence and power, Michael began to change how he managed meetings and how he used his body in social space.

The next time Michael gathered the leaders for a meeting, he decided to deliberately take up leadership space. He held the meeting in his home and arranged the group in a haphazard circle. He chose a comfortable chair and sank into it with a relaxed air. He began the meeting by sitting forward, looking at each person and speaking clearly. He told them what they were going to discuss and what decisions they needed to make by the end of the meeting. Then he sat back. Every time Michael wanted to make a comment, he would lean forward to speak. He made sure everyone had a chance to share their opinions. At the end of their time together, he brought the meeting to a close by summarizing the decisions and the assignments. One particular leader had been continuously sarcastic and critical during the meeting, so afterward Michael took him aside and told him the sarcasm had to stop. Michael said he would meet with him one-on-one to help him uncover what was motivating his negative emotions in the group.

After a couple weeks of practicing these new behaviors, Michael said, "I felt released. I felt free as a leader for the first time in my life. Who I was as a big guy with lots of presence was a good thing, not a problem. I wasn't embarrassed anymore by people looking to me for leadership. Instead I was serving them better than I ever had before by being a better leader."

PRACTICAL STRATEGIES FOR LEADING IN THE SANDBOX

Since influence is granted to you by others, how you handle your body in social space matters. Here is a list of specific and practical strategies for bringing presence to meetings and other social interactions. These come from research about the mechanics of influence and from my own personal experience.

Where you sit matters. Leaders usually occupy a central position, such as at the head of a table. However, if a leader doesn't take that position, it is better to sit across from rather than alongside the leader. In small groups, people direct more comments toward those they face rather than those to the side. People speak most naturally in face-to-face or corner-to-corner configurations. If the setting is friendly, there are more likely to be side-to-side conversations. If there are turf battles or power struggles within the group, those members usually sit farther apart. People tend to sit closer to those with similar attitudes. As distance decreases, openness and self-disclosure increases.

The term *Steinzor effect* describes how the directions in which people address their comments in a group is based on the level of leadership that is asserted.[1] If the leader is at the head of the table and gives minimal leadership, individuals will speak to those sitting across from them. The more space the leader takes, the more likely it is that group members will speak to those sitting beside them. If leadership is shared, neither pattern of conversation is observed more than the other.

People naturally interact more with the people they are looking at. The conference table, a piece of furniture found in most churches and businesses, has a leveling impact. Everyone is seated at about the same height and has a visible place at the table. Everyone is seen. The more important the discussion, the more important it is for everyone to have the same physical advantage.

Here are some general seating guidelines for group interactions:

- If the group is seated in a circle, sit across from the leader for easy eye contact.

- If the group is seated theater style, sit in the second row.

- Sit next to someone who has a different opinion than you.

- If you are the leader, you will encourage more shared leadership and participation by not taking the prominent seat. Arranging the chairs in a circle serves the same purpose.

- The more a leader needs to direct the meeting (e.g., in crisis management, conflict, vision casting or developing a team of lone rangers), the more important it is for the leader to take a prominent seat.

How you gesture matters. If you want to make a key point, lean forward and use palm-down hand gestures. Sitting back with palms open suggests a lack of conviction or submission to the will of the leader or group. People who take up the most space usually talk the most. If their body language is stiff and they point and speak in a loud voice, listeners are less receptive. People who take up less space usually speak in a quiet voice and use nervous gestures, such as jingling keys in a pocket or twirling a strand of hair. If a group perceives that a presenter is anxious, they will have little confidence in the presentation.[2]

The following nonverbal gestures communicate a lot about the person who is speaking:

- If a person is fearful, he or she exhibits flight gestures: keeping corners of the mouth back, pulling lips in, licking lips, swallowing

- If angry or disgusted, he or she uses assertive gestures: frowning, pointing, gesticulating, wrinkling of facial features

- If relaxed, he or she uses relaxed gestures: leaning back, settling in, neutral facial expression, laughing, folding arms

- If a person wants to draw attention to himself or herself, he or she will flash a smile, brighten up, rise up, nod, continue to smile

Strive for a relaxed, open and warm presence that comes from an inner confidence in your role and purpose. Despite the level of your role authority, your body communicates whether or not you believe you have a part to play in the discussion.

How and when you speak matters. When it comes to manner of speech, awareness of your audience makes a difference. Factors such as gender, age, ethnicity, personality types, local culture and group values impact how you should interact and initiate conversations about a topic.

J.D. was the newest and youngest pastor on the ministry team. He was hired as the pastor of family ministries. He discovered that the elders were mostly businesspeople who appreciated efficiency and accountability. The first time he took a proposal for a family retreat to the elders, he took a business approach, laying out the details of purpose, communication strategies, costs and time and place. The elders had a reputation for sending new proposals back to their originators two or three times before giving approval, but they were impressed with J.D.'s thoroughness. They understood what he wanted to do, why it was important and how it was going to get done. His proposal was immediately approved. J.D. was pleased, but he also knew that in the setting of the house church he had previously pastored, the members would have balked at such an approach to a new idea. Knowing your audience is good leadership, not manipulation.

Take risks in conversations to initiate your ideas and perspectives. Initiating conversations about your convictions, both in meetings and outside of meetings, is a key mark of inner strength. Leaders are not afraid to share their thoughts or suggest a course of action. Whether or not the ideas get picked up by others is not the primary concern. Initiating ideas conveys to others that a person has creative thinking, awareness of issues and problem-solving skills. Some church environments encourage such initiation at every level, but others discourage it outside of proper processes and meetings. Regardless of where you are, speak up.

When you speak, avoid being overly dramatic or emotional. As you raise the emotional content of your tone, others begin to shut down or react. This is a special burden for women, unfortunately. Men are often given more permission to be emotional then women are. Speak using rational language, and avoid a defensive or accusatory tone. Words like *always, never* and *very* escalate the conversation to an emotional level, and it rarely helps.

Use "I" language when speaking about your own ideas and "we" language when representing a team's perspective, but be careful about this if you are a woman. I used to say "we" all the time when giving presentations, even when I was primarily responsible. I believed in teamwork and wanted to honor everyone's input. But I learned that because I'm a woman, people often assumed I was reporting for others rather than presenting. People paid more attention if I spoke clearly for myself.

Speak during discussions and offer an opinion, but don't wait too long or you may lose your opportunity. Bruce, the techie on staff at a campus ministry headquarters, learned this too late. After a heated meeting about the technology needed for the ministry to maintain its website and Internet capabilities, Bruce voiced his opinion to Kurt.

"I don't think we're thinking creatively enough or broadly enough about the future directions of technology as they relate to faith."

"Why didn't you speak up in the meeting? I kept expecting you to say something, but you didn't!"

"Well, everyone was so into it and had such strong opinions. I just didn't know how to jump in."

"You just jump in. You just start talking. If they don't hear you, wave your arms. Say, 'Hey, I have a thought or two!'"

"I didn't want to upset anyone."

Bruce found that his reticence to speak up led to poor decisions by the group, and he had to live with the consequences.

If you speak and get cut off, do not react but wait for the person who interrupted you to stop talking. Then say something like, "That's interesting. I'd like to finish my thoughts," and then finish them. You may get cut off if you are going on and on about something. It's best to speak clearly and simply for just a few minutes. Using words to fill up space rarely influences people's thinking, especially if the discussion involves something controversial.

Don't end sentences using the same kind of inflection as asking a question. For example, "Well, I think this is a good idea?" or "I'm not sure if you understand?" You begin making a statement, but when the inflection goes up at the end, it sounds like you're asking a question. Women in particular do this so they don't seem pushy, but it gives the opposite effect, making it seem like you're unsure. Avoid disclaimers such as "I'm not sure myself, but . . . " or "I'm not an expert, but . . . " or "I've never done this before," or "I'm really nervous, so . . . " People get caught up in your excuses, and your influence capacity is diminished.

Make your opinion clearly known three times, and after that, let it go. Even if something really matters to you, present it no more than three times in a meeting.

Todd was sure that doing a message series titled "The Iraqi War: God's War?" was really the wrong decision for his ministry team. He knew that the majority of the congregation would understand the pastor's intent, but he also felt in his heart that using the pulpit for political purposes was not a good idea, no matter which side you were on. Todd spoke his mind three times during the discussion on the leadership team. Each time, he tried to take a different approach that would help the team understand the issues involved. Each time, he was ignored. So he let it go.

Unless you are in charge of a presentation or conversation, try not to speak first or last. If you are an extrovert and feel comfortable talking in a group, make it a point to listen to several others before you say anything. As an extrovert, wait for two to three people to speak before each time that you speak. Be aware of others in the meeting and don't take up more than your fair share of space. If you are an introvert, discipline yourself to speak at least once every meeting. Barney was an introvert, so he dreaded the regular check-in time at the beginning of meetings. They allotted thirty minutes for the three members of the group to share what was going on in their lives and make prayer requests. Martin always started and almost always talked for twenty to twenty-five minutes (Barney clocked it). Debbie went next, taking five to ten minutes. Then Barney, the introvert, would say a couple of things in the last two minutes. Barney decided he would take the initiative to start the sharing time, and he would make himself talk for ten minutes. After a couple of meetings, he began to enjoy the opportunity to share who he was with the other two. Most surprising to Barney, however, was that they never complained about the change.

If you already have little influence, speaking first puts you in a vulnerable position. It's interesting to me that Jesus did not speak first in the encounter at Simon's house. When you speak first, those who disagree can dismantle your ideas. On the other hand, if you have a lot of influence, speaking first makes it difficult for others to offer contrary opinions. Speaking last to summarize the meeting is a strong position. Speaking last to get the final word and stay in control is a misuse of power.

Keeping personal boundaries matters. Resolve not to lose yourself in a meeting. Andy learned this the hard way. He came to a meeting feeling relaxed and happy about how his day had gone so far. But then Tom brought up the issue of how kids had trashed the church gym when Andy led an overnight event there a month ago. Andy was really sorry he hadn't made arrangements to restore the gym to its previous clean condition. He was sorry the building caretakers had that extra work to do before Sunday worship. Andy had apologized profusely. Now Tom was bringing to the meeting a major policy change about the use of the church's facilities. Andy felt humiliated in front of the other leaders. He had a hard time remaining detached because he felt like everyone was criticizing him.

When a meeting triggers strong feelings in you—such as anger, inadequacy, shame, embarrassment or frustration—it's important to pull back and discern what is going on internally rather than get involved in the discussion. If you need to step out briefly to pray and think, then step out. If you can't leave the meeting, stop participating in the discussion and do the internal work of sorting out your feelings. Strong feelings are attached to deeper issues and can indicate opportunities for growth. If you cannot unpack them or get clarity during the meeting, ask if the discussion can be tabled until you've had some time to reflect. If the group is comfortable with each other, you might say, "Can we stop a minute? I'm angry right now, and I'd like to understand what is going on with me. Can we back up, and maybe you could help me unpack what's going on inside of me?" If it is a safe group, most people will welcome the opportunity to help another person grow.

Know your role in the group. Sometimes enthusiasm gets ahead of reality. Gary was new to the campus ministry team, and he was very excited about being involved with the inside decision-making and planning. He had all sorts of cool ideas for getting more college students involved in Bible study groups. At his first meeting, his enthusiasm got the best of him, and over and over he interrupted Jeff, who was leading the meeting. Gary didn't notice that people were getting uncomfortable. Finally Jeff said, "Gary, I love your enthusiasm. Thanks for all you ideas and energy, but you're interrupting our team processes here. Why don't you just listen for a couple of meetings and watch how we interact with each other and do things. After that, let's talk and you can let me know what you observed."

Having boundaries matters, but respecting the boundaries of others is also important. We can get carried away thinking about our ideas and forget our responsibility to serve as a host. A host brings a spirit of hospitality to every conversation. Everyone gets to eat. We don't take the serving bowls and meat platter and empty them onto one plate. Neither do we take food off someone else's plate. We listen. We try to understand what each person brings. We invite others into the discussion. If other people get cut off or are not given space, call on them, whether you're the leader or not.

Being prepared matters. Stepping into the sandbox also involves coming prepared for the business at hand. This is especially significant if you are bringing a proposal or want to offer a different view on a controversial issue. Here are some tips for bringing something to the table:

- Get input from everyone who would be affected by the change. It never helps to surprise people with decisions that have repercussions for them.

- Seek the wisdom of others who have had experience with a similar proposal. Talk to other spiritually centered leaders to get their take on the situation.

- Touch base with the person chairing the meeting and let him or her know ahead of time what you are bringing and how much time you need.

- Prepare to communicate your ideas without criticizing, judging or attacking the efforts of others. The more inflammatory or controversial the issue, the more important it is to write out clear primary points beforehand.

- Understand the theological and biblical issues involved. Give careful attention to how your proposal relates to things that matter the most, theologically and biblically, in your ministry setting.

- Come to the meeting with any tools, statistics or books that support your point of view. Are there key books, articles or websites to refer others to for information about the topic or issue? Bring stats and resources that handle the subject fairly, with good scholarship.

- Bring at least two options to explore. It is often difficult for a group to imagine things differently from how they've always been done. It takes time for prayer and wild "why not?" thinking to jump the neural networks to new channels of thought in our minds. Bringing more than one option to a problem stimulates people to think creatively rather than simply react.

JENNIFER'S STORY

Jennifer was the creative arts director at a fifteen-hundred-member church in Southern California. She felt that Eric, the operations director, was out to get her. He ignored her whenever she saw him, and he complained to the pastor about her. She had started an interpretive dance group, something Eric had strongly objected to. The pastor believed in Jennifer and had allowed her to start the group despite opposition from Eric and a couple of elders. But now the breakdown between Eric and Jennifer was the elephant in the room whenever the pastoral team met. The pastor called a meeting to pray about and review the dance group proposal once again.

This time Jennifer put herself in Eric's shoes and tried to imagine what was so difficult about the issue for him. She did her homework on the biblical and historical contribution of dance to spiritual life. She chose not to use emotional language but instead connected dance to the mission of the church. She made eye contact with everyone present, not just the ones who agreed with her. Instead of doing the presentation from her chair, she stood at the head of the conference table. She did what she could to take up space as a servant leader.

Jennifer began her presentation by having the pastor tell the story of how he changed his mind about interpretive dance in worship. He shared that while attending a church leadership conference, he saw an interpretive dance of the biblical story about the persistent widow pleading with the judge to take up her case. The pastor was so moved, he committed himself to having the heart of the widow rather than the judge. The pastor now believed others might have a similar experience.

After the pastor spoke, Jennifer presented her information and proposal. She anticipated and addressed possible concerns about types of music, dress and dance movements. At the conclusion of her presentation, Eric asked some probing questions. When Jennifer responded well to them, Eric removed his objections. He also saw Jennifer in a new way. She wasn't just a young, artsy type who didn't value the sacredness of worship; she was a creative leader who cared about the church.

Jennifer figured out how to take up space as a leader despite opposition, and it worked for her. However, even with the most noble of purposes and lots of prayer, preparation and intentionality, taking up space does not mean things will work out well. Most of the time, but not all the time, people are reasonable and will pay attention if they experience you using your power well, taking up space for servant reasons.

Leadership at the top is lonely. A leader often becomes a lightning rod for dissatisfied and broken people. Sometimes more power means you are less known. Even when you are managing your power and presence well, leadership is a complex business. If you step into a leadership environment, and despite your best efforts things get worse rather than better, I recommend this spiritual discipline: whenever you enter a hostile or unhealthy space, make it a conscious moment of stepping into sacred space. When you step into sacred space, you are on deck as Jesus was— sacrificially, with love, for the sake of God's kingdom and others. Create a short prayer to use whenever you find yourself in such places, something like, "Lord, with you and like you, in this space I serve."

The difference between stepping into sacred space and entering secular space is one of attitude. You can be in the center of a church's life and still be completely in secular space. In secular space, you protect yourself and your agenda or react to others and their brokenness. When you step into sacred space with Christ, then no matter where you are, what is going on or who you are with, the mission of God's kingdom is at the forefront. You are attached to the heart and mind of Christ. You notice your emotions and deal with them. If you are angry and want to hurt others or you are fearful and want to run, you stop and pray so that you stay in sacred space. Thoughtfulness about our influence matters because the kingdom of God matters. It is not trifling to pay attention to our bodies and the power we exercise in community. This attentiveness is part of kingdom hospitality.

QUESTIONS FOR DISCUSSION

1. Think of a meeting you attended recently. Where did you sit? With whom did you interact? Who talked the most? The least? Have you ever deliberately changed your behavior in a meeting?

2. Share a time when you brought something important to a meeting. How did it go? Did you use any of the practical strategies given in this chapter? Would you do it differently today?

3. What other practical tips do you have?

4. What should you do if you follow all the guidelines given here but it doesn't make a difference?

12

THE GUARDIANS

Overseeing a Leader's Use of Power

**Let the elders who rule well be
considered worthy of double honor.**
1 TIMOTHY 5:17

> **We treat space somewhat as we treat sex.
> It is there, but we don't talk about it.**
> **EDWARD HALL**

ANNA'S STORY

A female student in one of my classes shared with me the following
story:

In the late nineties, I was in the United States for a year of furlough from missionary work in Argentina. As was the policy
for missionaries on furlough, I attended the annual meeting of
my denomination known as Council. I looked forward to the
meeting with great anticipation because one of the issues to be
discussed had to do with women in ministry. A study commission had been formed the previous year to bring to Council specific recommendations that would then be brought to a
vote.

I went to Council prepared to speak to the issue from the
floor since the outcome of the vote would affect me personally.

Not being accustomed to the subtleties of political maneuvering, I was taken very much by surprise when I perceived that the discussion from the floor had nothing to do with the issues per se, or with the nature of the recommendations. Rather, the purpose of the discussion was to effectively keep the study from ever coming to a vote. Pastors utilized their power very strategically and effectively through *Robert's Rules of Order* to such an extent that those of us who wished to speak to the issues felt utterly impotent and powerless to change the direction of the session. The real issues were never brought to a vote, and the study in essence became meaningless.

Later at the closing Communion service, some of these same pastors, dressed in their Sunday suits, formed a solid line on either side of the Communion table. They had used their power exceptionally well during the discussion on women. Now we were supposed to see them as servants, offering the broken body and poured-out blood of Christ to the church. I found it to be one of the most distressing scenes I've witnessed, imprinted deeply on my memory because it graphically demonstrated the difficulty surrounding the issues of power and authority.

BRINGING POWER OUT OF THE SHADOWS

Anna's story is a sad example of what happens when leaders use their position to accomplish their own agendas. Whether the pastors agreed with the study recommendations or not, the way they maneuvered the meeting to avoid the issue was power used poorly. These things happen when a culture has no language or protocols for discussing power. Leaders at the top don't have a way to approach the use or misuse of power in their system. This includes denominational leaders, leaders of large parachurch or mission organizations and leaders who develop or supervise other leaders. I doubt that the pastors serving the body and blood of Christ to their Christian sisters thought too much about what they had just done. It felt wrong to Anna, but there was no way to name and evaluate how power was being used. Denominations, Christian organizations and churches of every kind need a way to bring power out of the shadows.

Besides not having systems and formats for observing power, the misuse of power is rarely seen as a significant mark of poor leadership. If a leader is "godly" (meaning that he or she is faithful according to the spiritual standards of the group), if a leader speaks well and inspires, if a church or Christian organization is "successful"— the misuse of power is rarely challenged. Since the important business of the church is to bring people into a relationship with Jesus Christ, to help them mature and to make a difference in the world, such problems within the system are frequently ignored. Yet the abuse of power is often the deal-breaker for many who leave ministry or the faith.

In our humanity we avoid talking about the misuse of power for various reasons. We think if we ignore the problem, maybe it will go away. Or we're afraid that if we do talk about it, it's too risky. Matters might get worse or we might lose control, and then we'd have chaos. Or we minimize the issue by rationalizing: everyone messes up now and then. Leaders need to lead, so don't interfere with "small" relationship problems. But this ignores the long-term damage that the misuse of power causes. In effect, these excuses mean that the misuse of power is not as important as saving souls, passing the budget or preparing for the next worship event.

Power is directly related to our identity, our sense of value and purposefulness. So power used well is potent beyond imagination. Power used poorly corrupts individuals and communities. It breaks down relationships. Power used well is transformational. Therefore, leaders at the top have a special responsibility to guard and watch over its use. That is only possible through concrete plans and processes.

CREATING A CULTURE ATTUNED TO POWER AND INFLUENCE

To be intentional about a group's use of power means to create a culture where power and influence are frequently discussed and evaluated. Bringing it up once a year for a check-in conversation is not enough to change the system. The more diverse and complex the organizational structure of a group, the more difficult it is to bring cohesion around new goals and directions. Simply adding an assessment tool for an occasional check-up on the leaders' and group's use of power is not enough. Power awareness can't be created with a program. It must be embedded in the culture.

Culture is "the way of life for an entire society," and it goes beyond the obvious elements of language, dress, religion and rituals, which are easily observable from the outside. Culture is intrinsic and is cultivated in the norms of behavior.[1] Simply saying that something matters or advertising it everywhere or having ball caps with a slogan on them does not mean that a group lives it. The true culture is observed in the normal ways people behave. For instance, a family can say that it is loving and present itself that way to the public, but if the behavior of the family members in the privacy of their home is unloving, the fraudulent culture will eventually break down. In more complex cultures, such as a megachurch, a national parachurch organization or a denomination, the norms of behavior have to be intentionally brought into the group's culture as actual norms, not slogans. Following are some guidelines for accomplishing this.

Mission-critical at the top. The concern and time invested in the stewardship of power and influence happens at the highest level of the organization. Changing how a culture perceives and uses power is most effective, perhaps only effective, when the primary leaders make it a priority. They are the ones who have the position and the authority to create initiatives or conversations that will happen throughout the system. These leaders create a vision for the importance of creating safe, energizing leadership settings at every level, from top to bottom. If the top leadership role is more of a positional-managerial one rather than one of authority, then the leader would use his or her moral authority and communication platforms to stir up the need for paying attention to the use of power. If this issue gets relegated to a taskforce that the top leader isn't invested in, there is little hope of imagining systemic change. If this issue is seen as someone else's problem in the system, it will have little substantive impact.

Modeled at the top. Talking about the need to steward power and setting up resources for using it well is only as effective as the extent to which primary leaders embrace it in their own lives. Brian McLaren is an internationally known figure and the author of many provocative and popular books on the church and leadership today. What I enjoy most about McLaren is his presence. When people ask questions, even when they are mean or critical, I've never seen him lose his relaxed body posture. He doesn't raise his voice. He doesn't smirk or become arrogant. He stays warm and relational. He keeps himself open to hearing the individual with careful consideration. He is one of the most nonreactive public figures I've meet in a long time. Whether you agree with him or not, he uses his presence well to host a conversation rather than to deliver dictums.

The benefit of our multimedia age is the ability to get closer to our leaders and have more exposure than ever before. With some leaders, we discover that there is a disconnect between their walk and their talk—or their writings. One man who wrote an enormously popular book on transformation was speaking to a select group of pastors before the main session of a conference. During that time he made several stereotypical jokes about his wife's nagging and shopping habits. Because of that, I have a hard time hearing him now— and this was only one experience. How much greater is the impact of a leader's presence on those whom he or she is around day in and day out. If you as a leader have people around you who consider you a bully (or a pansy), it will not be possible for you to change how your culture sees and uses power. It begins with those at the top seeing it and living it out.

Lived at the bottom. Leaders at the top create a culture where the ethos of empowerment to influence has the same potency throughout the system. In the same way that conversations and changes happen at the highest levels, they also happen at the lowest. One national organization spent two years and hundreds of hours changing how the system managed its schedules, ensuring that everyone took two days completely away from work to be with their families. However, the support staff was still expected to get their work done even though the majority of them had to take work home over the weekend. If it matters at the top, it has to matter throughout the system. At the lowest levels, the stewardship of power more likely means taking up space rather than managing it. Will the system allow for voices at other levels to influence decisions at the top? Will the system make sure that what matters at the top also matters throughout the structure?

Common language about power and its stewardship. When an organization wants to make a major change, the leaders create a common language that everyone uses. This gets everyone on the same page. Usually this takes the form of slogans or phrases that embody the essential message of change. I visited a church in England that had success in restoring persons whom other churches and the social system hadn't helped. One of the key features of this church was that the culture of transformation had its own language, which permeated throughout the system at every level. The same phrases were used over and over again in everyday conversations as well as focused ones. Whether a person was new or had been there for years, they all knew the church's language of change. And the behavior matched their language.

The same is true when introducing change concerning power. Language about power and its use is found throughout the culture. Language shapes us. Therefore a common language about power will shape individuals and groups. This book is meant to catalyze conversations about power and influence so that leaders develop a language that works in their settings. In order to create a language in your setting, you (1) use the same words and phrases consistently in every context, (2) create retreats or experiences where the concepts get internalized into language use, and (3) continue honing the terms until they are universally understood throughout the culture. If they have to be explained over and over again, you're not there yet. You need more training and clearer language.

An important part of every culture's language is the stories and metaphors that represent that culture. For instance, a cross in the front of a church identifies that place as Christian. If a church tells stories about people coming to Christ or making a difference in their local community, then the values of the church have been translated into real experiences. Everyone who knows and cherishes those stories belongs to that group in some way. If a pastor or denominational leader shares a story of how he or she recognized his or her use of power and used it well, it is more memorable than talking about it as an abstract idea. In the same way, metaphors for using power well help the group visualize or imagine how power is expressed and used in the culture.

Importance of diversity when evaluating power. When a group is homogeneous, it is harder to visualize the way power is used. People are comfortable with each other and with the way the system works. The faculty at George Fox Evangelical Seminary where I teach is like that. We've been together for several years. We have some amazingly loud and invigorating discussions about all sorts of things, from atonement theology to whether or not a certain course should be required. I don't think any of us are very good at seeing how much space we take up because there is no challenge to it. However, when I'm talking with laypeople in my church about a decision that needs to be made, my voice carries a lot of weight. I have to be mindful how my presence impacts the discussion.

In a less homogeneous environment, I am more likely to see my true self, not my comfy self. One of the reasons I really enjoy my church is because it is so diverse, and I come upon my true self more often than I do in the classroom. That gives me an opportunity to grow and become more Christlike. I can see how I use power to bring other people along on the journey. Leadership teams that are all male or all female or all Latino or all white or all middle-aged or all young will not see clearly how they use power in that setting. If a group really desires a more Christlike attentiveness to how power is used, the group needs to be more intentional about creating diversity in its members.

Importance of equality in promotion and advancement. If the stewardship of power is an essential part of a system, then clear opportunities for people to change or advance in their responsibilities or roles exists. If the social power grid does not change, then discussing power is simply an act of stating what already is rather than imaging what it could be. That means individuals who want to and who have the capacity are given training opportunities. A person who shows gifting and wisdom, even if he or she does not fit the general group profile, is given opportunities to grow and develop as a leader. For example, if a Latino in a Caucasian environment begins to demonstrate gifts for leading, then he or she is given opportunities.

Who gets opportunities to be on a group's public platform, who is encouraged to get more education, whose voice contributes to the discussion—all are indications of whether someone is given more leadership space in that culture. If it is obvious to the group that only certain types of persons can sit at the head of the power table, then a discussion of the stewardship of power is fairly fruitless. It never ceases to amaze me that Jesus gave those at the edges of power opportunities to serve as his witnesses. I believe the church is called to do the same. It is this upside-down approach to leadership that marks the Christian organization or community as distinct from the corporate world.

Importance of sharing decision-making power. If a diverse group is to work well, then each person needs the chance to participate and be taken seriously in decision-making matters. This doesn't mean that everyone in a system needs to process every decision. It means that when important decisions are being made, those who are impacted have a voice. When important decisions are being made, the true use of power is on display for everyone to see, as in Anna's story.

A megachurch pastor shared a story of meeting a church volunteer in the stairwell. They were going in different directions, but the volunteer said hi and asked the pastor how he was doing. In fact, the pastor wasn't doing well. He had a major decision to make, and his team was deeply divided over it. The pastor told me, "Usually, I would have just said, 'Fine, and you?' and kept going, but I decided to stop and talk with him. The Spirit in me said to slow down and listen, so I shared what was going on, as much as I could. The man was quiet a minute, and then he said, 'Well, Pastor, have you thought about . . . ' and he laid out a new way, like a traffic controller laying out coordinates for a jumbo plane to land. I was amazed and deeply grateful." By giving that volunteer a chance to influence, it was the pastor who was helped, but it also had an impact on a man who was included, even serendipitously, in the decisions of the church.

Supervising and mentoring about power and influence. One of the most significant keys to infusing a system with healthy power dynamics is for the top leaders to mentor not only the promising pups from the same litter but also the ducklings that don't seem to fit but have leadership promise. Inclusion is a powerful experience. When you are a minority or different or new, being included is huge.

It makes a major statement to the entire system when persons in power mentor potential leaders outside their immediate professional and social networks.

If a person is to succeed in the environment as a leader, they need supportive supervisors.[2] This encourages growth and allows for feedback. *Feedback* and *supervision* are tough words to hear sometimes because they imply evaluation, critique and adherence to standards. However, authentic supervision is done by someone with experience who cares about your success. He or she is there to give support and feedback and to make sure that you don't crash and burn but actually thrive. Supervision is a relationship of support and guidance. For the sake of God's kingdom, it is critical that we have someone giving us honest and helpful feedback. Otherwise it is difficult to really know how we are perceived in a group and how we use our bodies to influence.

360-degree feedback on power. One form of feedback is the 360-degree method.[3] In the corporate world, this method gives people a chance to get input not only from their supervisor but also from their peers, from the people they serve and from themselves. Full-circle, 360-degree feedback is effective when based on observable behaviors, not on opinions about how much someone is liked. It's helpful to get feedback on how others experience us because we usually aren't aware of that when it comes to power dynamics.

For instance, a person who feels like a victim will bring a victim mentality to a team experience. Victims can take up a lot of space projecting their pain onto others. Donna had been physically abused by her father as a girl. While working as director of development at a Christian university, Donna often felt like people were out to get her. She tended to personalize it when other people were having bad days. On the other hand, Dennis, the director of admissions, was used to getting his way and wasn't aware that he often came across as dismissive and arrogant in team meetings. Both Donna and Dennis loved their jobs and wanted to make a difference in people's lives. However, neither was aware of how their past was tattooed onto their presence.

The university where Donna and Dennis worked did 360-degree feedback as part of their leadership assessment process. Donna discovered that her staff loved working with her, but they were weary of her emotional overreactions to their innocent or stupid mistakes. They felt they had to tiptoe around her. When Donna realized she was carrying a victim mentality into team meetings, she sought a spiritual director to help her find inner healing from her past. She also asked her team to let her know when they were feeling stifled. Dennis also had a 360-degree evaluation. When he found out how others saw him, he was defensive and hurt. But he moved past it and took the feedback under advisement. He apologized to his team and requested that if they feel dismissed by him in the future, they come to him for a conversation about what transpired.

Several authors suggest that focusing on a person's strengths is much more helpful than focusing on weaknesses.[4] This is one of the reasons Dennis was able to do the hard work of paying attention to how he influenced. The feedback showed him that his team respected his leadership strengths, including seeing a clear picture of the future, being able to communicate that to them and breaking it down into manageable steps. He realized that they valued him, but he needed to treat them with respect. A year later, his team reported that they felt safe with him and appreciated his growth as a leader.

The value of effective 360-degree feedback is that it also helps the team develop. Because the feedback isn't coming from just one person, the whole team has the opportunity to manage how they work together. Instead of seeing feedback as something about the individual, it is about how the group interacts. Until people have an opportunity to talk openly about that, power might either be used poorly or underutilized by persons abdicating their influencing role in the group. Feedback also gives teams opportunities to have conversations about how they are relating as a diverse community, whether the differences are issues of gender, culture or roles.

STEWARDING POWER AS A CULTURE

To change the system, leaders with the broadest band of influence and control must make the stewardship of power a high value in the culture. This is hard but important work. Last year we had a sprinkler system installed in our yard, which consisted of a mixture of Johnson grass, good grass and a wide variety of weeds. The installer dug up the front yard, laid the sprinklers, then tilled in the weeds and what little grass was left. He overlaid it with an organic chemical to kill the old grass and weeds. But it was late in the fall, so the rains washed away most of the chemical. When we planted the new grass seed, the initial growth was beautiful. But as spring rolled around again, up came all the weeds, clover and pesky plants that we thought were gone. The yard will have to be reseeded once again. Making a change in a culture requires a lot of work, both internally and externally. If we don't take the time to do the deeper work of tilling up the soil and incorporating a means to protect the culture and keep it healthy, the weeds will come back.

Jesus sacrificed his life so we could have a redeemed life together as his incarnate body. Therefore, it matters that the body has everything possible to thrive. The guardians, the leaders at the top, have the responsibility to watch over and protect the use of power in their organizations. They need to make sure we have (1) candid discussions about the nature of power and the use of presence to influence in meetings, (2) conversations about how each person perceives his or her presence, (3) diverse persons on teams to encourage the fullness of Christ's body, (4) regular checkups with leaders for giving and receiving feedback on how a person's presence contributes to the life of the body, and (5) a culture where openness and the prize of Christ are more important than control and protecting insecurities.

It is difficult today to serve as a denominational leader, board leader or leader of a parachurch organization or educational institution. Out of many important efforts, leaders must choose which ones to champion. However, power is a pivotal concern. It is inexorably connected to the issue of love. If love is corrupted, it is often because power is misused. Power is the soil that protects and nourishes the root system so that the tree grows strong and bears much fruit. If we pay attention to it, we can create a healthy environment where people feel free to be honest, risk growth and try on leadership hats to actively protect the fragile ecosystem of the church. The Holy Spirit, as the source of pure power, is unable to function if human pride, turf protection, weak egos or pig-headed stubbornness become the turnoff valve to this rich source. The highest levels of leaders are the guardians who create a perimeter of protection for power to have its redemptive place in a spiritual community.

QUESTIONS FOR DISCUSSION

1. How have you seen power used well by someone of significant influence? How have you seen power used poorly?

2. What kind of language about power might work in your setting?

3. How might your church (or ministry or denomination) train and mentor leaders in the use of power?

4. How might your church (or ministry or denomination) evaluate the use of a leader's power?

CONCLUSION

One Leader Makes Room

While honoring Steven Spielberg at the Kennedy Center on December 26, 2006, Liam Neeson said that when Spielberg was asked, "Which is your favorite ending?" he replied, "Hope."

Reading books and transforming lives: these two activities often sit on opposite sides of a great chasm. It's not hard to read something helpful or inspiring and to imagine how things could be different. It is very hard to integrate premises and ideas into real, everyday, have-your-coffee (or in my case, tea), go-to-work-then-to-bed life. But it is not impossible or even unlikely. Under the guidance and power of the Holy Spirit, pulling these worlds together involves both a decision and a process. As a leader, you first decide something truly matters, and then you begin an intentional and prayerful journey toward making it happen. In this case, it begins with deciding to influence as Jesus did and to use power redemptively. Then it's a journey of discovering along the way how that happens. There is choice, intentionality, creativity and the Holy Spirit on this journey.

The following story is a composite of several real-life experiences that illustrates the journey of a leader who wants to honor God with his life by using power well.

CHRIS'S LEADERSHIP JOURNEY

Recently Chris attended a seminar on power and influence presented at a national leadership conference. Afterward he talked to the presenter about some of his questions, but he wasn't sure he understood it all. Chris was in the middle of a confusing power struggle in his second church plant, and his difficulties brought up memories of his first church-planting experience. At that time, he'd been on a team with two experienced and gifted American Baptist pastors. Al and Jake had known each other for years as pastors in the same conference. They were accountability partners, and their wives were close friends. Chris was Presbyterian, inexperienced and the newcomer. It wasn't long before Chris figured out that his power quotient on the team was fairly low. Al told him, "You're not what we expected, Chris. We thought you would take care of the finances and administration. That's what Jake and I need." Chris decided to take the role of new kid on the block so he could try to learn and fit in as best he could. In hindsight he realized he didn't know how to take up space to influence well in that type of environment.

Chris discovered that working in the church was not like working in the business world. He'd sold medical supplies for ten years before going into ministry, and he was quite successful. But God called him into the ministry, so he went to seminary and then teamed up with Al and Jake. He enjoyed the fact that all the leaders of the church plant, both lay and clergy, were deeply passionate and invested in creating a church that attracted people to Christ. They believed it could happen, and in faith they all worked hard toward that goal. On the other hand, Chris found that working with Al and Jake was difficult. In the beginning, Chris would get angry and defensive when he was ignored during important discussions at their pastoral team meetings. Then he would just shut down. Sometimes he would mentally beat himself up about all the stupid things he was saying and doing. Sometimes he complained to a few of his own groupies, which he knew wasn't right or helpful in the long run.

It was frustrating and confusing serving on a team with Al and Jake. If Chris had an idea, it might be accepted but would be attributed to Al or Jake. If he disagreed with one of them, he was in for a long battle until he eventually caved. If he agreed, Al would often change his mind. Chris thought he was going crazy. Then he decided to bring up these problems more often in meetings. Chris became more forthright. This caused Al to amp up and Jake to shut down. Chris had long talks with the elders, and they seemed clueless about how to get help beyond telling the pastoral team to get their act together. Chris finally decided to try counseling, and that's when he began to see how his own dark nature was playing into the dark nature of the other two pastors. Whenever there was a conflict, Al became aggressive, Jake tried hard to please and pacify Al, and Chris got defensive and reactive.

Even as the outsider, Chris began to get more experience as a leader and a preacher. He was loved by the congregation, which led to more problems on the leadership team. Having three people at the top was too confusing for everyone. But because the three pastors kept their behavior professional, very few people in the church were aware of the brewing relational problems.

Finally, Chris knew he had to go. He realized the team would never get along well enough to prosper together. After three years, he left. Chris was sad but not upset. He knew it had been an invaluable experience. He learned a lot about church planting, preaching and working with volunteers. He grew a lot personally. He understood himself better. He focused more on Christ and less on his reactive self. He relaxed. He used more humor and took himself less seriously. He was different. He had done his inner work. He realized the part he played in creating an unstable leadership team. He had even gone on a retreat to sort out his bad feelings and anger toward Al and Jake. He felt ready to move on.

After a year, Chris moved his family to a different city and started another church with the blessing of his denomination. He decided to find leaders who were outsiders, marginalized in their current settings, and team up with them to plant a church with the vision of keeping healthy relationships with Christ and each other at the center of their endeavors. Now, two years into it, he felt he was back in the same bad dream. Already two leaders had left because they couldn't get along with each other, and now one of the remaining leaders, Ellen, was beginning to attack Chris.

Ellen told Chris that he wasn't listening enough and that he was influencing too much in the meeting times. She said they were all business and weren't taking time to listen to each other's hearts and to the Holy Spirit. Chris couldn't see what the problem was. He thought the meetings were going well and were even fun. But afterward he would get the call or the e-mail, accusing him of being overbearing and disagreeing with anything Ellen said. The tables were turned. Now he was the bad guy, but he just couldn't figure it out. He was tired of having all his energy consumed by relationship problems among leaders. And he seemed to be constantly at the center of it.

Chris had tried everything with this church plant. He tried being more of a "parent" leader, creating a safe environment for the others. That's when one leader decided to quit; he didn't want anyone messing with what he brought to the table. Chris tried being low-key and letting situations unfold without giving a lot of input or direction. That created confusion, and one couple finally said, "Just tell us what to do. We can't figure out what's going on here or what we're supposed to be doing." Chris then tried sharing leadership, but even when he was sitting on the sidelines, he was accused of giving too much input and undermining another leader.

What was wrong with him? Maybe he wasn't a leader after all. Maybe he should go back to selling medical supplies. He was really good at that. He was popular in that setting. And he made good money too. Maybe the power dynamics in a church were too fuzzy to really get a handle on them. Who is really the boss? Who gets fired if things aren't going well? How do you stretch people to give their hearts to God's kingdom purposes and pay attention to their own darkness at the same time? Chris felt like conflict was the mixing bowl, power was the beaters and he was the batter getting knocked around and around until he was blended into someone else's will.

Chris decided he needed to get away for much-needed prayer and rest. He didn't think he could hang in there much longer. He was sure the next e-mail complaining that he didn't say or do the right thing would be the last straw, and he would just walk away from the whole business. Not from Christ, but from the ministry of doing church. This wasn't what he signed up for.

Chris booked two weeks at a retreat center in Montana, as far away as he could get. He was grateful that his wife supported him, even encouraged him to go, though it was going to be tough financially and emotionally. His kids, in elementary school, said they'd be okay without their dad for two weeks if he'd call every night and pray with them before they went to bed. Chris couldn't wait to get in his car and head toward Montana, Big Sky country. The first few days, he was an exhausted mess. He walked and walked the trails in the open spaces of beautiful Montana. He loved watching the clouds over the plains in the late afternoons. He slept until his heart felt like it was alive again and the ache of failure eased up some.

Then Chris started praying in earnest. Not like he used to, begging God to tell him what to do or asking God to fix the situation. Instead, Chris would walk to a little meadow that still had wildflowers blooming, lie down and offer himself up to God. He didn't say much. He just brought his will and heart together, asking God to take them and make them into instruments of peace. He confessed his need to be right and his fear of failure. He gave to God the shame he felt for creating problems for others. He had begun to think that if he left the ministry, God's work would go forward better without him. Chris confessed this thinking as his own shame, not God's design.

During these times of prayer, Chris asked God to help him see what entanglements were impeding movement and holding the team hostage to the misuse of power. Had he really been creating a table for others to come and experience God in action? He honestly thought he had, but now he realized he didn't know for sure. He prayed out loud, "Lord, I know I am blind. Blind to my own nature. Blind to the subtle shiftings that take us down in meetings over and over again. I can't see, but I want to. I need to. Help me be your servant. Help me find a way."

Chris remembered a conference he had attended where Dr. Gordon Dames from South Africa had been a speaker on a panel. Chris dug out his journal and turned to where he'd written Dames's words: "We are the firstfruits of God's kingdom. If we cannot create space for peace, for re-creation, for dignity, for the fruits of the Spirit, where will people find God?"[1] Those words had pierced his soul when he first heard them, and they did again as he reread them. They represented his calling. He wanted to create space where people could find God, but here he was creating space where conflict was the norm. He thought back to the Scripture God had given him when he first felt called into pastoral ministry, a personal paraphrase of Isaiah 58:10: "If you give yourself to the hungry and meet the needs of the afflicted, then your light will shine in the darkness and your gloom will be as midday." Yet now it seemed that whenever he gave himself, he went further into darkness instead of light.

For the entire first week and part of the second, Chris would go out each day to the meadow, lie down, present himself to God and pray the same prayers. Each time he heard nothing, but he believed he was heard. Each time, he rose up from the meadow and headed back to his spare little room feeling rested and hopeful.

On the fourth day of his last week at the retreat, Chris sat at his small desk and began writing. Things started coming to him. A way began to unfold. He wrote whatever came into his head. He reviewed his journal notes from the power and influence seminar. First, he needed to take a power audit of himself. He had a lot of power. He had underestimated the impact his presence was having on the group. He wasn't the new kid on the block anymore. He hadn't given the others a chance to talk about his power and to talk about how they experienced it in the group. He needed to confess his leadership error of not stewarding this resource. The social power he had belonged to the mission of their faith community. The social power that each of the others had belonged to the mission too. It was not about him against them; it was not about him empowering them, or vice versa. It was about each one taking responsibility to uncover the secrets beneath the surface. It was about allowing the Holy Spirit space to speak and guide them when they were confused.

Chris knew he needed to put on the table the pattern of conflict and confusion about his power. He wanted his team to put on the table their own power struggles, placing them before Christ to receive his guidance. They would talk about it. They would pray about it. He was sure that at some level there was brokenness that needed to be named, whether conscious or unconscious. Chris wanted to create a culture where they would begin meetings not with personal journeys but with relationship journeys. How are we getting along?

How are we learning more about ourselves and others in the group by doing this amazing thing of planting a church together?

Chris decided to do an audit of the group's social power as well, so they could plan together how to steward it. If people on the team could not take responsibility for their own darkness, it was not worth damaging the mission of the whole for the darkness of the one. As long as everyone—including himself and beginning with himself—was humbly trying to figure out how to create a "space for peace, for re-creation, for dignity, for the fruits of the Spirit," they could get through this. It was like they were in a long-forgotten valley that most people did not know how to walk through, but he wanted them to commit to getting through the valley to the meadow on the other side.

Chris planned to take fifteen minutes at the end of each meeting to ask this question, "Did you feel drawn to Christ and Christ's mission today? If so, why? If not, why not?" Each person would write down two to three sentences answering the question. The answers had to be primarily about what was happening within them individually and within the group, not about criticizing or blaming someone else.

Before Chris could do all this, he knew he needed to ask one of the members of the leadership team to leave. Nathan had been with him for two years, but he was not onboard with the direction the church was going. Chris knew this was part of the problem. Nathan was not willing to do the inner work of unpacking how his own humanity was overshadowing the work of Christ in him. Ellen, on the other hand, was just inexperienced and confused, much like Chris was at his first church. He more than anyone would know how to mentor and support her on her leadership journey. Cal, the other leader on the team, was laid-back but deeply committed and a careful thinker. He would be a stabilizing force in the group. Chris knew that even though Cal was a great motivator and communicator, he could get overly reactive. Cal's face was like a movie screen spelling out everything going on inside his mind, and that tripped him up.

Chris needed to take more leadership responsibility for the group as a whole by paying attention to the Holy Spirit, to the group dynamics and to their mission. He had gotten distracted by getting things done. He wanted to develop a language for them so that they could discuss power at any time. Some phrases he jotted down were:

- "Time out. I'm in rabbit mode" (withdrawn, shut down).

- "Time out. I'm in lion mode" (aggressive, reactive).

- "That felt like space-taking power. Can we talk?"

- "Are you in the shadows? Want to talk?"

- "Can we come to the center?"

- "Are we feeling powerful or powerless?"

- "What is our social power?"

- "Are we using power to create a space for hospitality or consumerism?"

- "Are our eyes on Christ in the center? Is our identity and mission in Christ?"

After writing and thinking and praying throughout the day, Chris felt hopeful again. But something was still nagging him. He had some strategies and steps for getting to a healthier leadership environment, but he knew he was not quite there. He had to think about his own body in physical space. In meetings he would often "go into his head" and forget to pay attention to his body and the bodies of his team. He needed to break it down and take responsibility for how he carried himself, where he sat, what mood he presented to the group, how he engaged others with his eyes and face. Did he really listen to what each one was saying, or was he always moving to a decision? Was he jumping to conclusions, making assumptions, feeling he was always right? Was he too busy or too tired to listen to what was really going on in the group? To pay attention at that level, Chris knew, would be hard work, much like learning to write with his nondominant hand. It would feel awkward, but he had to slow down to listen. He wanted to observe the interactions and body orientations of the team. He was sure there was much more going on between them than he had realized. He added these question to his list:

- "How's your body?" (relaxed, connecting, tense or withdrawn)

- "How's *the* body?"

Chris decided to get back into restorative rhythms with God. With all the relational problems, he had neglected his morning times with God. He knew his energy and hopefulness came from the hour he spent each morning just hanging out with God, reading the Scriptures and listening for God's voice. He also needed others to pray for him and encourage him when he was feeling down. He had kept to himself too long. He didn't want to burden already overburdened people, and he didn't like the idea of confessing his feelings of failure, but he knew he needed to confide in one or two safe individuals. There was a saintly couple in his church, Hal and Ginger. Maybe they would meet with him for coffee on a regular basis to be his encouragers and prayer supporters.

Finally, Chris felt the team needed to do more fun things together, like go to a movie, share a meal together, hike, whatever. If he was worn down, the whole team would be. Play is a great leveling field for power because the focus is on enjoyment, not on work. Chris also needed to find a mentor or two, outside his church and denomination, who could help him unpack how he managed his power. Maybe that workshop leader could help him.

Chris knew that people are most influenced by hope. He had a responsibility to create a hopeful vision of the future by creating space that was safe, open and centered in Christ. Dietrich Bonhoeffer, Chris's spiritual hero, had been silenced four times but each time became louder. Bonhoeffer knew who he was in Christ. Chris had teetered on the brink of failure twice, but he could succeed with Christ. For the sake of others who had not experienced the hospitality of Christ's generous love, Chris could do this. He would do it. He was ready to go home.

FINAL WORDS

I've met leaders in churches, hospitals, prisons, colleges, crosscultural ministries, theological schools, businesses, social services—and I've never met one who, having already decided to love and follow Jesus, didn't want to do his or her very best. Leaders who are called by God want to be faithful. They want to be part of the Holy Spirit's movement in their places of service. No one plans to fail, be miserable or lead badly. When they go to bed at night, in their hearts they want to imagine the Lord saying, "Well done, good and faithful servant." But in leadership it doesn't take long to realize that it's a lot harder and more complex than you ever imagined. We fail—often. We are miserable more often than we want to be. And we lead badly and hurt people. Perhaps that keeps us humble, keeps us at the feet of the cross. But we can't give up. We need leaders. We need all types of leaders in all kinds of settings, from the first-grade Sunday school class to the presidency of a worldwide relief organization.

I honestly believe that learning how to use power is a core competency, second only to an authentic walk with God, that will have a catalytic impact on how we lead. Our bodies know this instinctively. Our bodies are messengers of the power story in each of us. In a group, our bodies fill in a canvas with many tiny strokes that are the allotments and usages of power in that gathering. Our use of power tells the story of our ability to love ourselves and others. God saw fit to create this world, like a giant sandbox, for us to play in and live in and work in together. He gave us bodies to house and give expression to our interior and spiritual lives. He gave us power as God's image-bearers to do greater works than Jesus did. And we can.

NOTES

Foreword

[1] As referenced by Jeff Taylor, "Unconnected Dots," in *Reason,* December 23, 2007.

[2] Or as defined elsewhere by Smith and Harper: "Signal. An act or structure that alters the behaviour of another organism," John Maynard Smith and David Harper, *Animal Signals* (New York: Oxford University Press, 2003), p. 15.

[3] John Maynard Smith, "Why Fruitflies Dance: The Variety of Reliability of Animal Signals," *TLS: Times Literary Supplement,* August 3, 2001, p. 11. For a full discussion see Smith and Harper, *Animal Signals.*

[4] Benjamin Franklin, debates in the Constitutional Convention, Philadelphia, Pennsylvania, September 17, 1787, as found in James Madison, *Journal of the Federal Convention,* ed. E. H. Scott (Chicago: Scott, Foresman, 1898), p. 763, and quoted in *Respectfully Quoted: A Dictionary of Quotations Requested from the Congressional Research Service,* ed. Suzy Platt (Washington, D.C.: Library of Congress, 1989), p. 66.

Introduction: A Leadership Journey

[1] Hall's ideas for understanding people's needs for different types of groups are presented in Joseph Myers, *The Search to Belong: Rethinking Intimacy, Community and Small Groups* (Grand Rapids: Zondervan, 2003), pp. 35-37.

Chapter 1: Bodied Influence

[1] Joseph C. Rost, *Leadership for the Twenty-first Century* (Westport, Conn.: Praeger, 1991), pp. 13-95. Dr. Rost reviewed the development of the concept of leader and leadership in literature.

Chapter 2: Holding the Dynamite

[1] The term was first coined by Robert K. Greenleaf in his 1970 essay "The Servant

as Leader" (Greenleaf Center for Servant-Leadership, [2008] <www.greenleaf.org/whatissl/index.html>). Larry Spears collaborated with Greenleaf on several books about servant leadership and wrote a well-known article on the topic ("Practicing Servant-Leadership," *Leader to Leader* 34 [fall 2004]: 7-11). Of course, the relationship of servanthood to leadership is found first in Scripture (Mt 20:25-28; Mk 9:34-35; 10:42-45).

[2]Rollo May, *Power and Innocence: A Search for the Sources of Violence* (New York: W. W. Norton, 1972), p. 35.

[3]Ibid., p. 99.

[4]J. P. French and B. Raven, "The Bases of Social Power," in *Group Dynamics: Research and Theory*, ed. Dorwin Cartwright and Alvin Zander (New York: Harper & Row, 1960), pp. 607-23. A more recent typology of power includes three categories: knowledge, position and presence or charisma (Angeles Arrien, *The Four-Fold Way: Walking the Paths of the Warrior, Teacher, Healer and Visionary* [San Francisco: HarperSanFrancisco, 1993]). However, the power of one's presence is determined by a combination of character and culture.

[5]Matthew White, "Death Tolls for the Major Wars and Atrocities of the Twentieth Century" (November 2005) <http://users.erols.com/mwhite28/warstat2.htm>.

Chapter 3: Simon and the Sinner Woman

[1]Marcus van Loopik, *The Ways of the Sages and the Way of the World* (Philadelphia: Coronet Books, 1991), p 7. N. H. Young in "Jesus and the Sinners: Some Queries," *Journal for the Study of the New Testament* 24 (1985): 73, finds no distinction between haburim and the Pharisees in the New Testament.

[2]Dr. Kenneth E. Bailey, a lecturer in Middle Eastern New Testament Studies and research professor of New Testament at the Ecumenical Institute (Tantur) Jerusalem, believes the haburim in gatherings were open to the public, though the public is assumed to be practicing Jews who would not be seated at the table. The public nature of these gatherings is discussed in *Poet and Peasant and Through Peasant Eyes* (Grand Rapids: Eerdmans, 1983), pp. 2-4 in volume 2. Also in *Jesus Through Middle Eastern Eyes* (Downers Grove, Ill.: IVP Academic, 2008) pp. 239-60.

[3]C. S. Lewis, quoted in Alan Jacobs, *The Narnian: The Life and Imagination of C. S. Lewis* (San Francisco: HarperSanFrancisco, 2005), pp. 181-82.

Chapter 4: The Epicenter

[1]John O'Keefe, "10 Reasons Why Your Church Sucks," ginkworld.net (2003-2006) <www.ginkworld.net/yourvoice/straighttalk/archive_2004_art/art_03012002.htm>.

[2]Cathleen Falsani, "Bono's American Prayer," *Christianity Today*, March 1, 2003 <www.ctlibrary.com/ct/2003/march/2.38.html>.

[3]Mahatma Gandhi quotes, ThinkExist.com Quotations (1999-2006)<http://thinkexist

.com/quotation/i_like_your_christ-i_do_not_like_your_christians/215104.html>.

[4]Maureen Kelly, *Creative Formation of Life and World* (Washington, D.C.: University Press of America, 1982), pp. 379-90.

[5]Jon L. Berquist, "Critical Spatiality," in *Imagining Biblical Worlds: Studies in Spatial, Social and Historical Constructs in Honor of James W. Flanagan*, ed. David M. Gunn and Paula M. McNutt (New York: Sheffield Academic Press, 2002), p. 26.

[6]Doreen Massey, *Space, Place and Gender* (Minneapolis: University of Minneapolis Press, 1994), p. 261.

[7]Edward W. Soja, *Thirdspace: Journeys to Los Angeles and Other Real-and-Imagined Places* (Cambridge, Mass.: Blackwell, 1996), p. 6.

[8]Massey, *Space, Place and Gender*, p. 251.

[9]Ibid., p. 265.

[10]Robert Forston and Charles Larson, "The Dynamics of Space: An Experimental Study in Proxemic Behavior Among Latin Americans and North Americans," *The Journal of Communication* 18 (June 1968): 109-16.

[11]Edward T. Hall, *The Hidden Dimension* (New York: Anchor Books, 1990), pp. 113-29.

[12]Hall, and those researchers who followed him, looked at these basic types of distances in various cultures from Western to European to Asian and Middle Eastern contexts. In this book I've used the Western understanding of space. It would look very different in other cultures. For instance, in Western culture persons in public space are most comfortable maintaining 12 to 25 feet of distance between each other. Westerners like to maintian a "bubble" of space between themselves and others. However, in Middle Eastern cultures space is not determined by proximity to other human bodies. Public space is open to anyone. If someone were to prefer where you are standing, they would simply move into your space hoping you would get the hint and move over. For them the invasion of space is not connected to the body, but to the ego. Therefore, pushing on someone's ego is far more aggressive than invading his or her personal space. Every culture has its own understanding of proxemics (Hall, *Hidden Dimension*, pp. 154-64).

[13]For a helpful and insightful book on teams, see Patrick Lencioni, *The Five Dysfunctions of a Team: A Leadership Fable* (San Francisco: Jossey-Bass, 2002).

[14]Allen W. Wicker, "Size of Church Membership and Member's Support of Church Behavior Settings," *Journal of Personality and Social Behavior* 13, no. 3 (1969): 278-85.

[15]Thomas Lewis, Fari Amini and Richard Lannon write about the power of close relationships to change and heal people just by their being together. They call it "limbic revision," or the effect of love to revise the brain toward health. See their book *A General Theory of Love* (New York: Vintage, 2001).

Chapter 5: The "It" Factor

[1]Michael Quinion, "Gravitas," World Wide Words (1996-2008) <www.worldwidewords.org/topicalwords/tw-gra1.htm>.

[2]John Kander and Fred Edd, "Mr. Cellophane," in *Chicago* (1975) <www.allmusicals
.com/lyrics/chicago/mrcellophane.htm>.

[3]I first found this phrase "the body is the message" in Aaron and Joan Wolfgang's
article, "Exploration of Attitudes in Physical Interpersonal Distance Toward the
Obese, Drug Users, Homosexuals, Police, and Other Marginal Figures," *Journal of
Clinical Psychology* 27 (1971), p. 510.

[4]For more on charismatic leaders, see Jay A. Conger, Rabindra N. Kanungo et
al., *Charismatic Leadership: The Elusive Factor in Organizational Effectiveness* (San
Francisco: Jossey-Bass, 1988); and Jay A. Conger, *The Charismatic Leader: Behind
the Mystique of Effective Leadership* (San Francisco: Jossey-Bass, 1989).

Chapter 6: The Law of the Jungle

[1]Susan Hanson and Geraldine Pratt, *Gender, Work and Space* (New York: Routledge,
1994), pp. 220-21.

[2]Dean's Committee on Women Faculty, "GRACE Project Final Report" (March 21,
2002), University of Arizona College of Medicine <www.medicine.arizona.edu/
grace/>.

[3]Linda M. Nilges, "I Thought Only Fairy Tales Had Supernatural Power: A Radical
Feminist Analysis of Title IX in Physical Education," *Journal of Teaching in Physical
Education* 17 (1998): 172-94.

[4]Dean's Committee, "GRACE Project."

[5]Aysan Sev'er, "Women, Men and Dominance in Small Groups: A Social Roles
Assessment," (Toronto: University of Toronto Scarborough Campus, 1990) <www
.utsc.utoronto.ca/~socsci/sever/pubs/dominance.pdf>.

[6]Cecilia Ridgeway and Chris Bourg, "Gender as Status," in *The Psychology of Gender*,
2nd ed., ed. Alice Eagly, Anne Beall and Robert J. Sternberg (New York: Guilford,
2004), pp. 217-41.

[7]Ibid., p. 237.

[8]Dorreen Massey in *Space, Place and Gender* (Minneapolis: University of Minneapolis
Press, 1994) argues that the approach of identifying things as dichotomies leads to
one being defined positively and the other negatively. If males and females are known
as two different entities—e.g., a male, "A," is different from a female, "not A"—the
male is the ordered entity and the female is the disordered one. Therefore, it is better
to define entities by the identity constituted through their interactions. Thus, both are
indispensable to making up the whole. Kevin Giles in *The Trinity and Subordinationism*
(Downers Grove, Ill.: InterVarsity Press, 2002) makes the same point, applying it both
to the Trinity and to relationships between men and women.

[9]Caitlin Friedman and Kimberly Yorio, "Working for a Woman Can Be a Bitch,"
Publishers Weekly (March 6, 2006): 82.

[10]Mana Lumumba-Kasongo, "My Black Skin Makes My White Coat Vanish,"
Newsweek, April 3, 2006, p. 20.

[11]Linton Freeman and Cynthia Webster, "Interpersonal Proximity in Social and Cognitive Space," *Social Cognition* 12, no. 3 (1994): 223-47.

[12]R. Roosevelt Thomas, *Beyond Race and Gender: Unleashing the Power of Your Total Work Force by Managing Diversity* (New York: AMACOM, American Management Association, 1992), pp. 106-7.

[13]Noel Castellanos, Bill Hybels, Soong-Chan Rah and Frank Reid, "Harder Than Anyone Can Imagine," discussion moderated by Edward Gilbreath and Mark Galli, *Christianity Today,* April 2005 <www.ctlibrary.com/ct/2005/april/12.37.html>.

[14]Valerie Barnes Lipscomb, "We Need a Theoretical Base: Cynthia Rich, Women's Studies and Ageism," interview, *National Women's Studies Association Journal* 18, no. 1 (2006): 3-12; and Toni Calasanti, "Ageism, Gravity and Gender: Experiences of Aging Bodies," *Generations* (fall 2005): 8-12.

[15]American Society for Aesthetic Plastic Surgery, "11.5 Million Cosmetic Procedures in 2005" (February 24, 2006) <www.surgery.org/press/news-release.php?iid=429>.

[16]Calasanti, "Ageism, Gravity and Gender," p. 8.

[17]Naomi Wolf, *The Beauty Myth: How Images of Beauty Are Used Against Women* (New York: Perennial, 2002).

[18]I. K. McKenzie and K. T. Strongman, "Rank (Status) and Interaction Distance," *European Journal of Social Psychology* 2 (1981): 227-30.

[19]Heather McKay, "Gendering the Body: Clothes Makes the (Wo)man," in *Theology and the Body: Gender, Text and Ideology,* ed. Robert Hannaford and J'annine Jobling (Leominster, U.K.: Gracewing, 1999), pp. 84-104.

[20]Debbie Maken, "Rethinking the Gift of Singleness," *Boundless Webzine,* January 19, 2006 <www.boundless.org/2005/articles/a0001199.cfm>.

[21]Elizabeth C. Evans, "Physiognomics in the Ancient World," *Transactions of the American Philosophical Society* 59, pt. 5 (1969): 5-28.

Chapter 7: Second Impressions

[1]Malcolm Gladwell, *Blink: The Power of Thinking Without Thinking* (New York: Little, Brown, 2005).

[2]Martin Seligman is a positive psychologist noted for his research on optimism and happiness. He and others, including Mihaly Csikszentmihalyi, Barbara Fredrickson and Charles S. Carver, study how people and communities thrive. (Positive psychology is the study of human happiness and optimal human function.)

[3]Interview excerpt with Martin Seligman on Optimism and Pessimism accessed January 20, 2008, at <http://www.learner.org/discoveringpsychology/12/e12expand.html>.

[4]Henry Cloud, *Changes That Heal* (Grand Rapids: Zondervan, 1992), p. 92.

[5]Peter Overby, "Body Language," *Morning Edition,* NPR, January 6, 2003 <www.npr.org/templates/story/story.php?storyId=903868>.

[6]T. Field, "American Adolescents Touch Each Other Less and Are More Aggressive

Toward Their Peers as Compared with French Adolescents," *Adolescence* 34 (1999): 753-58.

[7]See Rebecca Lipsitz, *Scientific American* (Sept. 2000): 32; see also William Chaplin, Jeffrey Phillips, Jonathan Brown, Nancy Clanton and Jennifer Stein, "Handshaking, Gender, Personality, and First Impressions," *Journal of Personality & Social Psychology* (July 2000), 110-17.

[8]I recommend reading their book to get a clearer picture of these dysfunctions; see Gary McIntosh and Samuel Rima, *Overcoming the Dark Side of Leadership: The Paradox of Personal Dysfunction* (Grand Rapids: Baker, 1998).

[9]See Daniel Goleman, *Emotional Intelligence: Why It Can Matter More Than IQ*, 10th anniv. ed. (New York: Bantam, 2005); see also Marcia M. Hughes et al., *Emotional Intelligence in Action: Training and Coaching Activities for Leaders and Managers* (San Francisco: Pfeiffer, 2005).

Chapter 8: Bean-Counting Social Space

[1]Adam Lisberg, "Massive Chip on Her Coulter" <http://sweetness-light.com/archive/the-daily-news-really-doesn't-like-ann-coulter>.

[2]Craig L. Blomberg, *Neither Poverty nor Riches* (Grand Rapids: Eerdmans, 1999), pp. 243-46.

[3]Bruce A. Malina, *The New Testament World: Insights from Cultural Anthropology, Revised Edition* (Louisville, Ky.: John Knox Press, 1993), 90-115.

[4]Douglas E. Oakman, *Jesus and the Economic Questions of His Day,* Studies in the Bible and Early Christianity (Lewiston, N.Y.: E. Mellen, 1986), 141-69.

[5]Bernard-Henri Lévy, "Fast Chat Road Trip," interview, *Newsweek,* January 23, 2006, p. 8.

[6]L. Shannon Jung, "The Shape of American Space," *Religion in Life* 44, no. 1 (spring 1975): 45.

[7]Maureen Kelly, *Creative Formation in Life and World* (Washington, D.C.: University Press of America, 1982), p. 379.

[8]Thad Sitton, "Inside School Spaces: Rethinking the Hidden Dimension," *Urban Education* 15, no. 1 (April 1980): 65-82.

[9]The settlement of the United States was at the expense of the original inhabitants, the First Nations people.

[10]Jung, "Shape of American Space," p. 44.

[11]Brian McLaren, speech given at Allelon conference (Eagle, Idaho, June 19-22, 2006).

Chapter 9: Space-Taking and Space-Hiding

[1]Carol Gilligan, "Mommy, I Know You," *Newsweek,* January 30, 2006, p. 53.

[2]Margot Morrell and Stephanie Capparell, *Shackleton's Way: Leadership Lessons from the Great Antarctic Explorer* (New York: Penguin, 2002).

[3]Dr. Timothy J. Keller, pastor of Redeemer Presbyterian Church in New York, quoted in Michael Luo, "Preaching the Word and Quoting the Voice," *New York Times*, February 26, 2006.

Chapter 10: Open Space

[1]Daniel Goleman, *Emotional Intelligence: Why It Can Matter More Than IQ* (New York: Bantam, 1995), pp. 148-63.

[2]M. Mitchell Waldrop, "Dee Hock on Management," Fast Company (October 1996) <www.fastcompany.com/magazine/05/dee2.html>.

[3]Tony Hendra, *Father Joe: The Man Who Saved My Soul* (New York: Random House, 2004), p. 181.

[4]For two excellent resources on understanding the relationship between our emotions and our spiritual well-being, see Peter Scazzero, *Emotionally Healthy Spirituality: Unleash the Power of Authentic Life in Christ* (Nashville: Thomas Nelson, 2006); and Dan Allender and Tremper Longman, *The Cry of the Soul: How Our Emotions Reveal Our Deepest Questions About God* (Colorado Springs: NavPress, 1994).

[5]Rick Ross, "The Five Whys," in Peter M. Senge et al., *The Fifth Discipline Fieldbook: Strategies and Tools for Building a Learning Organization* (New York: Doubleday, 1994).

Chapter 11: Getting in the Sandbox

[1]David B. Givens, "Steinzor Effect," Center for Nonverbal Studies (1998-2001) <http://members.aol.com/nonverbal3/steinzor.htm>.

[2]For more information on body language see Tonya Reiman, *The Power of Body Language* (New York: Pocket Books, 2007; and Allan and Barbara Pease, *The Definitive Book of Body Language* (New York: Bantam Books, 2004).

Chapter 12: The Guardians

[1]David Jary and Julia Jary, *The HarperCollins Dictionary of Sociology* (New York: HarperPerennial, 1992), p. 101.

[2]R. Roosevelt Thomas, *Beyond Race and Gender: Unleashing the Power of Your Total Work Force by Managing Diversity* (New York: AMACOM, American Management Association, 1992), 101.

[3]For more helpful resources on 360-degree feedback, see Adrian Furnham, "Congruence in Job-Performance Ratings: A Study of 360 Degree Feedback Examining Self, Manager, Peers and Consultant Ratings," *Human Relations* 51 (1998): 517-30; Joan Brett,: "360 Degree Feedback to Leaders," *Group and Organization Management* 31 (2006): 578-600; and Susan M. Heathfield, "360 Degree Feedback: The Good, the Bad and the Ugly," About.com: Human Resources <http://humanresources.about.com/od/360feedback/a/360feedback_2.htm>.

[4]Marcus Buckingham and Curt Coffman, *First, Break All the Rules: What the World's*

Greatest Managers Do Differently (New York: Simon & Schuster, 1999). "People don't change that much. Don't waste time trying to put in what was left out. Try to draw out what was left in. That is hard enough." Marcus Buckingham and Donald O. Clifton, *Now, Discover Your Strengths* (New York: Free Press, 2001).

Conclusion: One Leader Makes Room

[1]Dr. Gordon Dames, speaking on a conference panel at Allelon Summer Leadership Institute: Ministry in a Postmodern Context (Eagle, Idaho, June 20, 2006).